"Here is a gift to anyone who has ⸻ ⸻ ⸻ ⸻ ⸻ crossed a threshold, kneeled on the earth, planted a seed, secretly yearned for life and love and roots to take hold. Which is to say, all of us. *Paradise in Plain Sight* stopped me in my tracks and invited me to look into the backyard of my own life in a different way: with deep attention and radical gratitude. To read this extraordinary book — so brief in length, yet so magnificently deep and so transparently clear — is to remember that home is where I am and that what I need I have. A simple reminder, perhaps, but offered with such grace and eloquence in these pages that I find myself returning to them again and again, to hear Karen Maezen Miller's voice telling me what my heart knows."

— Katrina Kenison, author of *Magical Journey*

"A wonderful book on the heart of Zen, the heart of life."

— Roshi Joan Halifax, abbot, Upaya Zen Center

"*Paradise in Plain Sight* is a beautifully written book. I have enjoyed Karen Maezen Miller's writing for years, and this book is every bit as wise, insightful, and honest as her previous books. I highly recommend it."

— Sharon Salzberg, cofounder of Insight Meditation Society and author of *Real Happiness*

Praise for Karen Maezen Miller's *Hand Wash Cold*

"Miller uses daily household chores — laundry, kitchen, yard — to demonstrate timeless Buddhist principles. The skillful weaving of personal anecdotes, a few Zen terms, and acute insights — sometimes addressing the reader directly — distinguish this book from others in the genre.... This disarming book is full of deft and reassuring observations."

— *Publishers Weekly*

"A direct reminder that wakefulness lurks in the moments of everyday life, whether they are completely joyful or completely a mess."

— Susan Piver, author of *The Wisdom of a Broken Heart*

"Miller discusses how to accept the way things are and appreciate the simple, ordinary things of life.... A good starting tool for those seeking an alternative to both traditional self-help psychology and spiritual practices."

— *Library Journal*

PARADISE IN PLAIN SIGHT

ALSO BY KAREN MAEZEN MILLER

Hand Wash Cold
Momma Zen

PARADISE in PLAIN SIGHT

Lessons from a Zen Garden

KAREN MAEZEN MILLER

New World Library
Novato, California

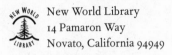

New World Library
14 Pamaron Way
Novato, California 94949

Copyright © 2014 by Karen Maezen Miller

Text design by Tona Pearce Myers

Library of Congress Cataloging-in-Publication Data
Miller, Karen Maezen, author.
Paradise in plain sight : lessons from a Zen garden / Karen Maezen Miller.
     pages   cm
ISBN 978-1-60868-252-2 (pbk. : alk. paper) — ISBN 978-1-60868-253-9 (ebook)
1. Spiritual life—Zen Buddhism. 2. Gardens—Religious aspects—Zen Buddhism. I. Title.
BQ9288.M55 2014
294.3'444—dc23   2013049005

First printing, May 2014
ISBN 978-1-60868-252-2
Printed in the USA on 100% postconsumer-waste recycled paper

New World Library is proud to be a Gold Certified Environmentally Responsible Publisher. Publisher certification awarded by Green Press Initiative. www.greenpressinitiative.org

10   9   8   7   6   5   4   3   2   1

Dedicated to Taizan Maezumi Roshi (1931–1995)

Dewdrops on a blade of grass,
Having so little time
Before the sun rises;
Let not the autumn wind
Blow so quickly on the field.
— DOGEN ZENJI

CONTENTS

PART THREE: LETTING GO
Make the effort of no effort.

PARADISE

One day when Buddha was walking with his disciples he pointed to the ground with his hand and said, "It would be good to erect a sanctuary here."
  — BOOK OF SERENITY, CASE 4

On a late Saturday afternoon in the early summer of 1997, after a string of auspicious disappointments and wrong turns, my husband and I found ourselves in the backyard of an empty house on a quiet street in a suburb of Los Angeles. The backyard was Southern California's oldest private Japanese garden, an oasis of ponds and pines that had stood mostly intact since 1916. It seemed like paradise with our name written all over it. We knew in our bones that the place could only be ours, and with it, the little house alongside it. The next day we put money down and a month later, we moved in.

The overwhelming certainty that we belonged there was soon followed by the overwhelming certainty that we didn't. Once we arrived, we hit the bookstores and local nurseries. We studied up on Japanese gardens: their esoteric architecture, history, and symbolism, and the very special ways to rake, weed, prune, plant, and water. We sought opinions, called in experts, and asked for conservative estimates — *ha!* — to redo this or that. The more we learned, the more we doubted. Perhaps we had overreached. It was too much work. It would take too much money. We were fools, without the right tools, training, or time. No wonder no one had wanted to buy this place but us. It wasn't paradise, but a colossal pain in the neck.

One day I ran across a single line in a thick book that made it all simple. It told the original meaning of the word *paradise* before it became a mythical ideal, imaginary and unattainable. Before it pointed somewhere else.

The word *paradise* originally meant "an enclosed area."

Inside the word are its old Persian roots: *pairi-*, meaning "around," and *diz*, "to create (a wall)." The word was first given to carefully tended pleasure parks and menageries, the sporting ground of kings. Later, storytellers used the word in creation myths, and it came to mean the Eden of peace and plenty.

Looking at it straight on, I could plainly see.

Paradise is a backyard.

Not just my backyard, but everyone's backyard. Teeming with weeds, leaves, half-dead trees, moles, mosquitoes, mud, dust, skunks, and raccoons. With a novice gardener and a reluctant groundskeeper.

Like the entire world we live in, bounded only by how far we can see.

I began to garden. I got scratched, tired, and dirty. I broke my fingernails and ruined my shoes. I yanked out what I could have kept and put in more of what I didn't need. I pouted and wept, cursing the enormity of the task. I was resentful and unappreciative. But when I ventured afield, sidelined by things that seemed much more entertaining or important, I always came back to this patch of patient earth. Time after time I realized that everything I want or need — the living truth of life, love, beauty, purpose, and peace — is taught to me right here, no farther away than the ground beneath my feet. I am a pilgrim, as we are all pilgrims, making my way through a paradise hidden in plain sight.

That's what this book is about: plain sight.

From the start, let me say that everything you will read here is a metaphor, and nothing is a metaphor. The best way to understand this is by not trying to understand. This book isn't really about Zen, and it isn't really about gardening. It might seem like I'm talking to myself, but I'm talking to you.

Now, about this paradise. You're standing in it.

For years, I've invited everyone I meet to come see the garden. And what I mean is to come see *this* garden. This garden that is your life.

It would be good to erect a sanctuary here. A paradise of your own.

Part One

COMING HERE

Have faith in yourself as the Way.

CHAPTER I

CURB
The View from a Distance

A monk asked, "What is the Way?" The master replied, "Stop standing at the crossroads gazing into the distance."
— THE RECORD OF TRANSMITTING THE LIGHT

First you have to find the garden. It seems far off, but it never is.

You will arrive at a place you've never been before, and you will enter it. Then you will come to see that your life is the life of the entire universe. You may wander off, but you will keep coming back. Eventually, you won't go anywhere else.

This is where it begins. It begins on the curb.

There is something haunting about looking into other people's houses. You can see the past and its long shadow of pain. You see wasted potential: ten thousand futures gone missing. You see a lot of stuff that no one needed to keep, do-it-yourself projects that should have been left undone.

You see what people love, and by their neglect, what they don't. You see a lot of bad carpet. On this day of house hunting, my husband and I saw nothing that we would ever want to inhabit.

The day had not gone well. More than a few days had not gone well. We were nearing the end of our second year of marriage and finally looking for our first home together. We had lived mostly apart, taking a measured approach to combining our single households in separate states. I wasn't happy it was taking so long, but my insistence triggered his resistance, and the gap between us widened.

That's what can happen when you're used to having your way.

We had met and married at the brink of middle age, each secure in our separateness, from entirely different worlds. He was an engineer, and I was a spiritual type. He was a loner, and I was a joiner. He believed in the metric system, and I believed in miracles. But the real difference was that I wanted everything to change, and he didn't, at least not yet. This kind of tension always surfaces between people, because for-and-against is a struggle we bring to everything we do. To prove it, just grab hold of what you think is your side of things, the *right* side, and tug. Wars like that can go on for — oh, I don't know — *forever*. You're putting all your effort into pulling a rope and then blaming the other side for the blister.

After barely a year of long-distance dating and then a fast-track wedding, I wanted to take up residence together, start a family before it was too late, and turn my world upside down. Sounds reasonable. But he wanted to take his time and have a plan. Sounds reasonable. Two reasonable people locked inside two different versions of reasonable: proof that reason alone doesn't bridge a divide.

In the last decade of the twentieth century, a two-career couple living in two parts of the country was called a marriage of the '90s. People marveled at our invention, but what I really wanted was a marriage of the 1890s. Barring that, I'd settle for sharing a zip code.

People who knew about our peculiar standoff would stammer in disbelief, "Didn't you decide where you would live, uh, *before you got married*?" The simple answer was no, and I blamed myself. I took great care, in my precarious approach to an impossible dream, to disrupt as little as possible in advance. Haven't you ever done that? Reached for something you want, on any terms, then seen that what you'd wrought was bent and half-broken, not quite working the way you'd thought it would?

I admit I had been less than clear about my intentions because they had been less than clear to me. Why did I, an independent, self-made woman, want to marry at all? Have a family? Willingly give up a last name, a job, and my own remote control to move across the country? With someone who was, for the most part, a stranger? To his credit, a benevolent one.

Because I thought something was missing in my life, that's why, and I didn't really know what. That's how we all live, as if we're missing half of ourselves, and whether we think that missing part is a person, place, or purpose, we call it our *better half*. Our *best self*. The *new me*. Even *happily ever after.* The best parts are nearly always the parts we think we don't have.

At least, that's how it looks from the curb, where we judge ourselves at a distance from everything and everyone else. We can stand on the curb for a long time, turn it into a crossroads from which every direction seems unappealing or even dangerous, afraid to take even a single step, so accustomed are we to feeling unlucky, unloved, or stuck. That day, I felt like all that, but I was about to get my way. Everything was about to change. It always is.

The feeling that we are separate — outnumbered and under attack — is where the spiritual life begins. It's the curb you have to step off of to get to the other side.

Sensing ourselves as separate is an illusion, but it's a crafty illusion. We're not separate at all, but it seems that way. It seems as if all our problems are caused by someone or something else.

We were kidnapped at birth and raised by strangers who never loved us. Misjudged by critics and overlooked by higher-ups. Unjustly accused and mistreated. The pawns of a system rigged against us. Ill-favored by fortune, betrayed by our friends, born too soon, born too late, in the wrong place at the wrong time. Undefended against an immutable force that's either standing in our way or running us over.

I'd been around the block a few times. Been stupid and wised up. Had it all and tossed it out. Made one plan and then another, then another. Lost in love and trusted someone again. And yet I was sinking into the pall of a malignant conviction — that I wasn't going to find what I was looking for, not today, not next week, maybe never.

That was me out there on the curb, looking into all creation, a many-splendored world arrayed at my feet, thinking *this isn't it this isn't it this isn't it.*

No matter what your story is, whatever your creed, you come to a spiritual practice looking for paradise. It's a paradise you've never seen yet feel as if you've lost. The question is whether you'll recognize it when you're staring it in the face.

You may not be able to change the way you think about yourself and the world, at least not in the first chapter of a book. But you can stop believing that all your thoughts are *true.* Because they aren't. There is another truth you may never have seen, and with it comes another way to live. It's called the Way.

From the curb you'll see the gate. From the gate you'll see the path. From the path you'll see the ground, and overhead, the sun and moon to light your way. These signposts will bring you to paradise.

We had exhausted our options by the time the agent drove us down one last street and surprised us by pulling over.

"Let me show you this one just for historical interest. It's empty, and you might not get a chance to see it again."

Whatever it was, I could hardly tell. The view from the curb was curtained by a stand of giant bamboo behind a rusted iron fence. Inside the fence was a worn-out gate.

Inside the gate was a weathered bungalow, faded to a forgettable shade of dust.

"I know it doesn't fit your parameters."

I wondered what she thought our parameters were. Fear? Distrust? Ambivalence? We had asked to see rental houses with short-lease terms, uncertain by this stage where or how we would end up. On the one hand, all bets were off. On the other, anything was possible.

Even from the street I could tell that this wasn't the rose-covered cottage I'd envisioned for my honeymoon haven. We were deep into LA's featureless sprawl, near where my husband worked, in a suburban hamlet known for its sooty skies and desert temperatures. I didn't know that there was something else my husband had told our agent to put on the wish list. Doubtful that his type A wife could survive having this much nothing on her hands, he had told the realtor that I might like a *little* garden.

The only thing I'd ever grown was mold on bread.

There was no little garden in sight.

And then she said something that shot me straight out of the backseat.

She said, "The whole thing was built for Zen."

. . . .

GATE
What's Holding You Back

The great Way is gateless,
Approached in a thousand ways.
Once past this checkpoint
You stride through the Universe.
— MUMON'S PREFACE, *THE GATELESS GATE*

In point of fact, the place was not built for Zen. It was built for vanity, the architect of most man-made things. But everything can be used for Zen once you get going.

The practice of Zen began nearly three thousand years ago when a man sat down under a tree in India and experienced enlightenment. His demeanor afterward seemed so uplifted that his friends called him Buddha, which means "awake." His teaching became a guiding light for wayfarers, who one by one and step-by-step carried it across the ground of many continents and centuries. People who practice Zen are more skeptical than some devotees. They want to prove the truth for themselves, and so they do what Buddha did. They sit down for long stretches. And then they get up and keep going.

Zen had already saved my life once. I had stumbled onto meditation during a dark period a few years earlier. The deep silence and discipline of the practice helped me get back on my feet. Without depending on special scriptures or doctrine, Zen meditation points directly to the truth of the human mind, which does not, by the way, mean the space inside your head. It means the universe beneath your feet.

So let's wake up and see where we are standing.

Just inside the fence was an oddly placed gate that wasn't really a gate. It was a wooden portal with swinging doors and a shingled roof. The frame was gnawed nearly hollow and slapped with peeling paint. It leaned to one side; the doors dangled, screws loose. It was old, that much you could tell, wobbly and cobwebbed, but as an obstruction, it seemed almost solid. Coming up to it, I stopped dead.

Where in the world am I going?

The agent was trying to tell us where we were going — onto old ground, what was once part of a larger estate, with a history and a bit of mystery. The gate had stood as the entry to a pristine garden, a side of the property we hadn't yet seen.

One hundred years earlier, a single woman of means, heiress to a timber fortune, had built a stately villa on this sunny hill. On the slope below, she planted three magnificent gardens as evidence of her worldliness — a Mediterranean garden with fountains, an English garden with roses, and a Japanese garden with rocks and ponds. This was the entrance to the Japanese one, the sole remaining garden, a relic of her once-charmed life.

In the early part of the twentieth century, Japanese gardens cropped up in quite a few unusual spots — in public parks and exposition grounds, on private estates, and, yes, even in some backyards. Since Japan had opened trade with the West in the mid-1800s, its culture had become precious, its art and aesthetics prized by the super-rich.

The woman who had commissioned the garden was simply doing what the wealthy do. She had fashioned a splendid fantasyland, but it did what everything does: it fell apart. When her investments failed, she parceled off her property and ended her days in a modest rental on the cheap side of the street.

Standing at the weathered gate, all we saw were the spiderwebs and the termite holes, and we were very afraid.

Fear is what holds you back from everything.

There's some lore about the gates outside Zen monasteries in the old days. Any seeker was refused at the gate until his intentions were clear. This might take several days or a week, each day the pilgrim making entreaties and the gatekeeper holding him back. What was going on there? Was this a way to screen out troublemakers and half-wits? No, there are plenty of those inside monasteries! Was it simply a show of rudeness? On the contrary, it was extreme kindness. Of elitism? Hardly. Anybody can enter. To pass the barrier, you have to drop your ambivalence and cynicism. Your clever self-deceptions, excuses, and ulterior motives. You have to be ready, even desperate, before you propel yourself beyond your own fear.

Then, of course, it's easy, because the gate isn't really a gate. Fear is a false barrier. It's nothing but a gaping hole you step through. On the other side, the teacher is waiting.

Four years earlier, I'd entered a different gate and met a great teacher. He had died, but while I stood at this threshold, he was not far from my mind. He was never far from my mind.

Taizan Maezumi Roshi was the product of an archaic system of Zen Buddhist patriarchy in Japan, where temples operated as family enterprises. One of seven brothers raised at his father's temple in Otawara, Japan, he was ordained as a priest at age eleven and studied literature and philosophy at the university. After that, he did two things uncommon for both his time and our own: he took his mother's last name, Maezumi, and he took the practice of Zen Buddhism seriously.

He'd lost respect for blind authority; he wanted to part with dead customs. After his institutional training, he sought instruction from radical masters, testing firsthand the truth of a timeless teaching. In 1956, at age twenty-five, he sailed for America, intending to spread the practice of Zen in a country hostile to both his nation and his faith. He was posted as a priest at a small temple in Los Angeles that served a diminishing and demoralized population of Japanese Americans.

His reputation grew. He attracted students from all over the world. He was revered by some, dismissed by others, and misunderstood by most. He was still there, in a dinky house in a dumpy part of town, on September 23, 1993, when I knocked on the door, afraid to say how afraid I was.

"I'm lost," I said, in so many words.

As if anyone got there any other way.

At this fragile point in my life I was between addresses, between careers, between marriages, between youth and the brittle aftermath of youth, beyond shame, without better judgment, and with nowhere else to go. But I'm not here to tell that story again.

He invited me to sit down, the very thing I feared most of all. It hardly makes sense that sitting still and quiet for eight hours a day in a meditation hall teaches you to stand up and put one foot in front of the other, but that's what Zen practice does. It is possible to traverse a great distance while your mind stands absolutely still. To alter your life entirely while doing next to nothing.

"Your life is your practice," he said to me, and it was true. My life had never moved farther or faster than it did after he'd taught me to sit down and let it happen. Now here I was in front of another gate, the cusp of a universe without fear. We all stand on a spot like this, every moment of our lives, facing the only universe we will ever know, and most of the time we turn back toward familiar haunts — the scary stories inside our heads. That's how we turn the gates of heaven into our own eternal damnation.

Is it even possible to live in a universe without fear?

I wish more people would ask.

Anxiety disorders are the number one diagnosis of the mental health industry. Each year, about 40 million American adults seek treatment for debilitating fear and dread. Now children are swelling their ranks. In one recent year, 85 million prescriptions were filled for the leading antianxiety drugs. Antidepressant use has quadrupled over the last twenty years. About one in ten people suffer from chronic sleeplessness. Deaths from prescription painkillers are epidemic and higher than those from illegal narcotics. There are 140 million people in the world with alcoholism. In America, heavy drinking is the third leading preventable cause of death. These numbers may not be completely accurate, but they are entirely true. If they don't apply to you, then they apply to people you know and love, people you live with or used to live with, people barely alive or dead too soon.

We live stupefied by our own deep terror, our unmet fears. Out of fear, we crush our own spirits, break our own hearts and — if we don't stop — rot our own flesh.

How do we end up like this? I don't know why we reach for noxious cocktails to drown our fear and pain, but we all do, and they don't work. Every time we turn away from what is right in front of us we are headed in the wrong direction. So don't turn away.

It's not easy. There are no shortcuts or detours. No one can tell you how to fast-forward your bliss. If they do, they're just making it up. I found out for myself that none of the secret formulas work. That's why I won't tell you how to fix a relationship, guarantee your happiness, or realize your passion. I can't repair your past or re-engineer your future. I don't know the alchemy that turns fiction into fact or pain into pleasure. There is no sure thing. I can only ask this: What are you ignoring? What are you resisting? What part of your life have you locked out and sealed shut? And I am not talking about something invisible and unspeakable.

Just take a look at what is right in front of you — the obvious and unavoidable — and step foot there. All that is ever required of us is that we lift one foot and place it in front of the other.

I didn't learn everything from that old teacher, but he taught me how to keep going, so I'll share that much with you.

When you come to the gate, keep going. Keep going straight on.

CHAPTER 3

PATH
Straight On

If you don't see it, you don't see it even as you walk on it.
When you walk the Way, it is not near, it is not far.
If you are deluded you are mountains and rivers away from it.
  — SEKITO KISEN,
      "THE IDENTITY OF RELATIVE AND ABSOLUTE"

You stumble along thinking you don't know the way, and then one day you realize you're in the middle of it.

From the gate, a cracked sidewalk pointed the path forward. It was the only slab of cement I'd ever encountered that gave me goose bumps — and not because we were in a wonderland. To the critical eye, the scenery was unspectacular: a suburban front yard with a few gnarled citrus trees and a weedy lawn. But there was something else at work. Something for me to notice.

The three of us walked under an arbor of fruit trees. Hundreds of ripe oranges bobbed overhead like ornaments. Here was a young Meyer lemon tree, its top growth shooting up to the sun. Clumps of blue agapanthus flowers flared open like starbursts. In the shade of the house, skinny-legged nandinas waved their lacy leaves and berries. A ten-foot-tall *Tibouchina* released its purple flowers like a swarm of butterflies. Mind you, I didn't know the names of these beauties, except for the fruit. I wasn't yet the gardener. I was the guest, but with every step I felt more at home.

This mind is an amazing thing. It can conjure love from the scent of orange blossoms, peace from a dry breeze, and joy from a patch of grass on a summer day. Until I was twelve years old, I'd spent nearly every weekend at my grandparents' house in the middle of the Ventura County orange groves about an hour north of Los Angeles. There, I felt adored. I didn't question whether or not I deserved it. Every memory of those days is infused with the smell of sandy dirt and orange essence. I'd spent nearly every summer at my other grandparents' house in the middle of the farmlands of Central Texas. There I played. I never once thought I was wasting time. Memories of those days are infused with the feeling of thick grass under my bare feet. It was all coming back to me.

Why are childhood memories so vivid? So real and lasting? Perhaps because as kids we pay attention to what's in front of us, undistracted by things we haven't done and places we've yet to go.

Finally, near the front door, two grapefruit trees, scarred and knotted with age, bowed low with the weight of their long labor. The fruit fell at our feet like a housewarming gift. I already knew it was my house. The last ten yards had convinced me I was right where I belonged.

The realtor was saying things that realtors say when clients are too quiet. I couldn't hear a word over the rhythm of my heart, pounding *this is it this is it this is it.*

There is such a thing as home, and the relief you find there is complete. All you have to do — for one flickering instant — is notice.

I'd always thought that a path was a means to an end. A course of study, a tour of duty. The distance from A to B. The anguished span between wanting and having. The truth is, I expected this second marriage to deliver me to something better — a happy ending. Zen too I'd seen as a necessary pit stop on the way to a higher realm. But as long as we're only passing through, we never arrive. The path isn't the way to *get* something; the path is the way to live.

It's a path we never leave but rarely even see. We don't notice where we're standing. We don't notice where we're walking. We don't notice the sights, smells, or sounds around us. We don't notice our traveling companions or the people we pass by. When we are absentminded, the world is a wilderness.

But all the while, we are on the way. That's what I knew for sure as I shuffled along, suddenly alert to every sensation. I knew that all my late starts, wrong turns, and missed signals were part of my path. Every lapse in judgment, miscalculation, and hesitation had been perfectly timed. Everyone I'd ever known, everything that had ever happened, had landed me here. Nothing I'd ever done had been a mistake. Not even the mistakes had been mistakes. It was like setting down a suitcase. No, more like crawling out of a shipping container that is packed solid with pain, guilt, blame, and regret. You don't want to get trapped in one of those. You'll never get out alive.

When I was growing up we used to snicker about my dad and his hankering for road trips. He would plan for days or weeks, map alternate routes, fill the tires, top the tank, load the car, and wake us in the dark to start the drive so we could get there — wherever there was — ahead of schedule. And then he would be perfectly miserable in the place and with the people we had come to see. These trips always ended the way they began: uncomfortably early.

When he quit working, he retired to a trailer in the woods, then to a house by a lake. His last try was a cabin in the mountains. Near the end of his life, he started one last road trip across the country to visit me. He never made it. He stopped at a hotel an hour from my home and called, asking me to come up and meet him for lunch. After a hamburger and a side of fries, he hugged me in the parking lot, turned around, and drove back the twelve hundred miles he'd come. His affliction was no longer a quirk; it had overtaken him. There was no place on earth he could rest.

Recalling it now, I don't think less of him. I don't think he was so different from anyone else. His curse is mine and yours too. The road is merciless when the company you can neither keep nor avoid is your own. And yet, by degrees of habit, this is how we live, until we learn how to make ourselves at home wherever we are.

❧

What do you practice? Whatever you practice, you'll get very good at. Some people become more fearful or cynical; some more arrogant or vain; some greedier; some needier;

some more combative or close-minded. That's what they practice.

And then there are a few who grow as solid as a mountain and as wide-open as the sky. They are strong and yet tender. Steady yet yielding. Powerful yet gentle. You will recognize them because they resemble the earth you can touch and the sky you cannot contain. It's not that they are superhuman; they are more *completely human* than most of us ever allow ourselves to be.

The people who knew me probably thought I had lost my mind the first time I walked into a Zen temple. And it felt like I had. That's okay, because you do not come to Zen unless you are lost. You do not find the Way unless you've lost the way — and I mean utterly lost, without hope of finding the route on your own, because only then do you have the momentary good sense to stop and ask for directions.

Formal Zen practice consists of sitting, standing, and walking around. Beginners expect to learn a high and holy way to perform these rites, and so they ask questions. The instruction goes like this:

How do I sit? Sit.

How do I breathe? Breathe.

How do I stand? Upright.

How do I walk? On your own two feet.

You cannot imagine the freedom and personal empowerment that arises just from resolving these issues.

Everyone has a path in life — including the spiritual aspect of life — and the good thing is, you don't have to find it. You are already on it, fully equipped for the trip. The path you are on always leads you farther on, in the same way you were led here today. To walk the path, you just keep going, asking, seeking, finding, and this is the most important thing: trying. If you haven't yet recognized your path it's because you haven't gone far enough to see clearly. We have to use our feet to get close enough for anything to come into focus.

"How did you choose Zen?" people ask me, assuming I made a deliberate choice to take the most outlandish path toward spiritual liberation. One answer is that I didn't choose. I simply followed the path straight ahead, and the way was made clear. The first step makes the next step simple. The second step makes the third unavoidable. By that point you begin to realize something profound about your life: there is no other way but the one you walk on. So you keep walking, trusting your own two feet, amazed at the way the scenery changes.

The other answer may sound weird. I really liked the way Maezumi Roshi walked: his bare feet padding across a polished wooden floor. Granted, he didn't look like much — he was a scrawny fellow, no taller than me, wearing mended clothes. You might suppose it is some grand philosophy that draws us to the spirit — a theory of the cosmos — but it is the feet, the hands, the eyes: this measly scrap of human life. Luckily for those of us with a wayward sense of direction, a Zen retreat consists largely of following in the footsteps of the person who stands in front of you. I was mesmerized by Maezumi's sure, elegant footfall, silent beneath the swoosh of his black robe. He moved, when he moved, like Kilimanjaro. I would have followed him anywhere. I guess you could say I did, although it led no farther than my own home. Once you admit you are lost, everything you see is a sign pointing home.

"Have faith in yourself as the Way," he said to me, and so I'll prop his words here, like a sign.

In a certain sense you could say that Buddha was homeless. He made a home wherever he went. He and his disciples were itinerants, each possessing nothing but a robe and a bowl to beg for meals along the way. In some Buddhist countries today, this practice has been ritualized into a monastic tradition. Monks pass through the monastery gates each morning and into the "real" world where strangers fill their bowls with offerings. The lesson is not one of poverty or humility. The purpose is not to instill charity or even gratitude. Buddhist rituals have no secret or special meaning, except to point directly to the true nature of our minds.

Each of us walks along a path with no sign of where we've been and no knowledge of where we'll end up. The earth rises to meet the soles of our feet, and out of nowhere comes a gift to support and sustain our awareness, which is our life. Some days the gift is a bite, and some days it's a banquet. Either way, it's enough.

Can you give yourself totally to the reality of your life and its unknowable outcome? When you do, the questions of where, when, how, and if will no longer trouble you. You might feel instead the ecstatic certainty of having *arrived*. That's what happened to us after we crossed the curb and passed through the gate that afternoon. We'd driven off the map and set down our list of criteria, entering the unfamiliar and lapsing into an unfiltered state of awe.

For years after this day we would see it happen again, as we invited groups of tourists and teachers, schoolchildren and gardening buffs, to walk through the gate and see for themselves. They came from distances near and far, in buses and carpools, in slow trudges uphill from the schoolyard, leaving behind whatever had come before — the spilled milk, the pop quiz, the god-awful traffic — with no expectation of what would come next. Right inside the portal, before anything splendid had been fully revealed, our guests would grow instantly calm, slow their steps, and form themselves into a saintly single file moving straight on, straight on, a procession of mendicants in silent reverie.

Seeing the transformation I would wonder, "Where do they think they are?" and then see the answer for myself. *Here.*

Here is the place; here the Way unfolds.

CHAPTER 4

GROUND
Here It Is

A monk said to Kempo Osho, "It is written, 'Buddhas in the ten directions. One straight road to Nirvana.' I still wonder where the road can be." Kempo lifted his staff, drew a line in the ground, and said, "Here it is."
— THE GATELESS GATE, CASE 48

Like most folks who come to Los Angeles to float their dreams, we couldn't avoid hitting bottom. We were already standing on it. Five million years ago, seismic storms pushed the Pacific seabed to the surface of the earth. The ground beneath LA is a basin of ocean sediment up to six miles deep. We were walking on a primordial floor, treading a path as old as time.

The first known homeowners in this valley were a tribe that wandered west from the desert fifteen hundred years earlier. They called themselves the Tongva, or "people of the earth." First conquistadors stole their sovereignty in the name of distant kings. Then Spanish clergy corralled their souls in the name of salvation. Soon little remained of the people but the earth for which they had once named themselves.

The era of ranchos followed, the common earth divided into vast bequests of land and water to loyalists of Spain or Mexico. Land grants could make a man wealthy one day and poor the next. Property claims were expensive to protect. Cattle prices often collapsed overnight. Family holdings disintegrated. Eventually, ranchos were sold off piece by piece to American settlers, who planted their own ideas in the dirt. Some of the schemes took root, and California blossomed into an agricultural utopia, producing the world's most exotic and abundant crops. One was the almighty orange. Citrus groves covered three hundred thousand acres across Southern California until the competition got too steep and the population too high. Then the orchards were plowed under to make way for suburbs.

I must have been walking on air when I wondered aloud about the street we were on. How did it come to be named after the capital of Peru, the City of Kings, with its mystical history and colonial grandeur? The agent let me down gently.

"Around here we pronounce it like the bean." This was an agricultural valley, and there had once been a lima bean farm down the road. I was mildly deflated.

Gravity always has the last word. Sooner or later we all come back to earth. Here it is.

❧

Until the day I landed on Lima Street, I was most comfortable — if you could call it that — at thirty thousand feet.

I liked being up at cruising altitude, with nothing weighing me down. I did my best thinking when my head was in the clouds, or so I thought. Pursuing love and money, I'd logged enough frequent-flier miles to earn my vaunted Silver Elite status. Like most of the privileges you earn with the swipe of a credit card, it was bogus. A hundred thousand miles of air travel would get you five inches of legroom and a few cashews along with your peanuts. Oh, and a seat farther forward in the plane, where you would be among the first to die.

They gave you a plastic luggage tag to signify that your bag of socks and underwear would be tenderly placed at the top of the heap. And the thing is, you believed it.

While I was up above it all, my problems seemed smaller. Daily strife seemed distant. The earth seemed orderly. Other people were irrelevant. Except for the crying baby two rows back, it was as close as I could get to heaven. But there was more to my peripatetic lifestyle than business or pleasure. I was seriously invested in the idea that life was a climb, so the feel of the ground meant two things: either you were just starting out or you were crashing into a steaming heap of pilot error. Settling on the ground was not for me, not for long. I was so afraid of ending up nowhere that I spent much of my life ascending, quite literally, into nowhere.

Consider the ways we situate ourselves in this world: by ranks of self-improvement and self-importance, attainment, worth and grade, by code and bracket — not to mention your boarding group. There is that invisible ladder of success you're supposed to scale, the ceiling you aim to break, and a nonexistent bridge or two to cross. We buy into these pretenses as proof that we've moved up, gotten ahead, and gone places. Separated ourselves. Distinguished ourselves. Made something. Meant something. Amounted to something. Lived a life that mattered.

As long as we think like that, we don't have an inkling of what life is, or where life is, or who we are. As long as we think that this great earth is merely something we pass over en route to some Silver Elite Jetway in the sky, we don't see that this earth is itself the unsurpassable way. You can't grab hold of anything higher than what's ready-made for you right here, where the glories unfold at your feet, ungilded lilies in the field.

After Maezumi died, I took up practice with a new Zen teacher. He observed me hopping from one place to the other, and he was pleased I'd be taking up permanent residence in California. He said, "This will be good for you. It will ground you."

Thinking twice about what he said, I took offense.

Was he saying I was a lightweight? A fly-by-night? Did he mean I wasn't serious? A part-timer, a half-timer, a short-timer? A kook, a fruit, a phony? Is that what he thought of me? Were my shortcomings that apparent? I *knew* it!

That's the problem with thinking twice. From a standing start, we propel ourselves thirty thousand feet off level ground and into the clouds, where we can no longer see straight.

I needed grounding. I always need grounding. When you get right down to it, it's good to be on the ground, where you don't have to wonder about things.

What ground? The only ground, silly.

The point of Zen is to settle on the ground. Feet, knees, butt: on the ground. Sure, we use a cushion, a mat, a bench, or a chair, whatever works, to ease us onto the ground. There is no Zen that is not on the ground.

The physical form of seated meditation is called the *mountain pose*. It looks just like it sounds. Sitting on a cushion or chair, the body is anchored in the earth and the head supports the sky. A mountain is what we imitate, but the more we practice sitting like a mountain, the more we *become* a mountain. Sitting, standing, lying down, and walking about: the mountain is unshakable but moves whenever it wants.

How does it move? Pick up your foot and stomp the earth.

With strength like a mountain, you can keep your eyes, ears, mind, and heart open. Light comes in, and you see things as they are. You see that the sun encircles you, the moon follows you, and the clouds disappear by themselves.

What clouds? Exactly. What clouds?

Maezumi Roshi used to say that Zen was misunderstood because it was so plain. A line in the ground: here it is. Embellish, and you've muddied the mark.

But you'll only see it when you stop looking for it.

I had walked down the aisle twice, and I knew how to turn back. Now the path was leading me to another altar, one with a porch and a front door. It was the altar of home, where the beloved is the earth and the vow you make is to stay. It's a hard promise to keep, but it is exacted from every last one of us, even if we don't deliver until we die and turn to dust. Could I commit?

I was not that far removed from a generation that lived

totally by the grit and grace of this earth. One grandfather grew fruit, the other kept sheep. These were not high-minded men. They were simple and sometimes crude. And yet they were not restless; they found their daily purpose in the light that fell between dawn and dusk. They sniffed weather on the wind, prayed for rain, damned the drought, brought forth families, buried kin, and stayed put. This last bit I attribute to something other than a lack of initiative: call it trust. They trusted the root to bear the fruit, the sheep to grow the fleece, and the sun to burst open blooms too numerous to count. Their lives were plain and hard: they worked the ground. There were no cashews in their pea-nuts. There weren't even peanuts.

With all my getting ahead, I thought I'd improved on their sorry lot. I thought I'd exceeded their meager dreams. In the end I'd traveled a long way to see what was keeping me airborne: avoiding the real work of planting myself on the ground.

Here it is.

༄

A survey is published every now and then that reports on the Most Popular Places People Would Choose to Live. Reading the results, you see that the most popular places are fantasy destinations: California, Hawaii, and Florida. But then I noticed that the question asked is not, "Where would you choose to live?" but "Where, *except where you live now*, would you choose to live?" If they asked the latter, they might not have a poll at all. Perhaps people would say, "You know, the winters are abominable and the summers are wretched, the streets are potholed and the neighbors are strange, but I'm fine right where I am." The poll is asking the same ridiculous question we ask ourselves: Where, oh where, is the grass greener? The answer is, Only in our fantasies.

There is no other place than *the one where you live right now*.

One time a radio host interviewed me about meditation as an antidote to dissatisfaction, and she seemed alarmed by this idea. Staying put runs contrary to the religion of self-gratification.

"It seems to me you're telling people to settle," she said, on air. Her scorn at that word, *settle*, unsettled me. I sputtered a response not worth remembering. If I'd had the sure-footedness of my kin, I would have said what I meant.

I would have said, "Yes."

We settle in the sheep turds because that's where the fruit trees grow. And with a little work, the fruit tastes pretty damn good! Some people settle with a field or flock; some with a stick or shovel; and some on a bench, chair, or cushion. Once you learn to settle the mind, you can settle anywhere and begin to cultivate the scenery. Then you might realize that the ground of your mind is the very ground of this earth, where your feet find the path and the future appears in plain sight. It dawns like the faint glow of an early morning. Even before you open your eyes, you know it's the sun.

CHAPTER 5

SUN
What You See

The blue sky and bright day,
No more searching around!
— Mumon's Verse, *The Gateless Gate*, case 30

And then I saw the garden.

I'm going to choose my words carefully here. Not because the garden is hard to describe, but because I want you to see it.

Sometimes people come to the garden and say, "It's so much smaller than I thought." Or, "It's so much bigger than I thought." Or, "It's not at all what I thought." They have created a picture in their minds of what the garden looks like, or what it should look like, and when they see the real thing they aren't seeing it at all but comparing it to a picture in their minds. We cherish the pictures in our minds. We prize our fantasies, or they wouldn't be our fantasies, perfected with every wish. Nearly everything we cherish is just a picture: our ambitions and ideals (a perfect size 4 or 6 or 8); our notions of what happy families and their homes should look like (not this); the past, the future; our vision of love, lovers, and life ever after. The picture might even be a nightmare — frightening and forlorn — but we cherish it just the same.

Sometimes people come to the garden and say, "I had no idea." Then they don't say anything else, because they are seeing the garden. They are seeing what is right in front of them and experiencing it. Then nothing needs to be said.

I had no idea what to expect when my husband called me to the kitchen. By this time we'd entered the house, and because it was empty, we did not take offense at what we saw. Empty rooms are full of possibility. Possibility is full of love.

"You should see this," he said.

I stepped into the kitchen, where he stood at a plate-glass window, looking out.

And then I saw the garden.

I saw a multitude of iridescent greens. The glint of sun-bleached stones. Red bark and burnished branches. The sheen on still water. Light on a hill. A foreground, a background: the seamless whole of three dimensions. Colors with no names because I wasn't naming them. Beauty beyond measure because I wasn't measuring it. A view unspoiled because I wasn't judging it. The shine of the sky making everything visible, everything vivid, even the shadows, with the radiance of being *alive*.

This was not a picture of a garden. This was not a

picture I could ever conjure from memory or make-believe. This was true life, so unexpected it made me cry.

When you see your life, you bring it to life. When you don't see your life, it seems lifeless.

"Do human beings ever realize life as they live it?" That's a line from the play *Our Town*.

And the answer is, "No. The saints and poets, maybe they do some."

The awakened mind has two attributes. One is compassion, what some would call love. The other is clarity, what some would call sight. They are not really two things. Each is a function of the other. When you see, really see, you just love. When you love, really love, you just see. You see things as they are, not as you expect, and in that wide-open space is love.

This is the kind of love that everyone wants, the kind that everything needs. It is love at first sight, unconditioned by definitions or demands. Nothing can come in between the pure seeing, not even a hairbreadth of difference, judgment, or hesitation. Not the filter of so-called understanding or an extra layer of elaboration, just the streaming of light unhindered by what you might otherwise stop and think.

Realizing this isn't hard. It sounds like a once-in-a-lifetime event, but it can happen at any time. Look up and see the light from the sun. And now see everything beneath it, everything around you. You are in the garden.

But do we ever realize it? No. Saints and poets, sometimes.

"We love it," we told the realtor, who suggested we

see the other rooms just to be sure. The bathrooms needed work.

❧

Soon after I met Maezumi Roshi I had a dream. My dreams at the time were rich and provocative. Sometimes they scared me. Often they confused me. But they were always illuminating. The life I'd assembled was falling apart — my first marriage, my career, my home, and my mental health — but my subconscious life was like a construction site. Deep beneath the surface, something new was growing, and I could see it almost every night when I closed my eyes.

In the dream I was sitting in the family room of my parents' house. With me were my mother, Roshi, and my father, who was sleeping on the floor. Everything about it seemed familiar: it was my own home, after all. And here was everyone and everything together. As in life, my father was the one we tiptoed past.

I loved being there, but I had to attend to something, urgently. I had to go to the bathroom. So I went into the bathroom, closed the door, and sat on the toilet. There was a window in that dream room, and I looked out of it to see Roshi and my mother walking on a sunlit path outside the house. Although they'd never met in real life, their pairing seemed perfectly natural: my earthly mother and my spiritual father, arm-in-arm. More than anything, I wanted to join them, but I had a job to take care of, the work we do in a bathroom: ridding myself of my shit.

There are people who bring you into this world, and there are people who show you the way through it. Ones who teach you what to do and ones who teach you what not to do. My mother and Maezumi Roshi had led me to this window, this kitchen window, and beyond it, to a dazzling path where I could join them. It was the place where the loving earth meets the brilliant sun: a real-life garden.

It is possible to know things without ever knowing how. One day you set down the picture and wake up to the truth. No more searching around.

Clarity is the essence of wisdom. Clarity alone, and not pie-in-the-sky beliefs, is the basis of Buddhism. In Zen language, the truth is continually manifested as *thusness*, which means "as it is." Everything, everywhere, is just as it is. And yet we argue it to death.

You might read that and think, "That's it? That's all there is to it? Isn't that obvious? Isn't there anything more?"

Yes, yes, yes, no. See how hard it is to settle for the obvious? It's so *obvious*.

As a word, *thusness* may seem like a conceptual abstraction that has nothing to do with your life. But it's not. Maezumi Roshi said thusness was the most complete, well-defined dharma, or truth, that we live. It is a truth intimately carried down by all spiritual ancestors — the intimacy of simply being yourself where you are and as you are. There's nothing more to it: nothing to get, nothing to gain, nothing to explain.

And while it is obvious, it cannot be understood. Face it: life cannot be intellectually grasped. You can't outwit creation, but luckily there is no need for that. Just by being, you surely know it clear as day. Being and knowing are the same; just ask the saints and poets. They manage it beautifully without wasting a word.

In fact, going on like this just adds troublesome clouds to the sunshine, so let me get back to the obvious.

The paint was peeling, the roof was shabby, the closets were tiny, and the bathrooms needed work. One of them was pink. But nothing else we saw — no ifs, ands, or buts — could overshadow what we'd seen at first sight. We told the agent to draw up an offer to buy it *as is*. Then we drove away feeling as if we'd taken title to a dream come true.

It was a really good feeling while it lasted. And then nighttime came.

CHAPTER 6

MOON
What You Don't See

When one side is illuminated, the other side is dark.
— DOGEN ZENJI

It was black that night, the moon a waning slice in the sky. I know because I stayed up worrying. I couldn't see how everything would come together. There were too many missing pieces.

Once I got back home again, I'd have to walk away from my job. Sell or shutter my business, cancel contracts, and let employees go. Get out of my lease, pack up the closets, call a mover, and give things away. Say good-bye to my friends and family, my income and identity, my reputation, and the status quo. As for gardening, I didn't know my ass from a hole in the ground.

The property had been on the market for two years, with no takers among a parade of lookers. Surely they'd seen something we'd overlooked — the labor involved, the limitations, the pink bathroom. The last would-be buyer had bailed just two weeks ago. The garden was beautiful, but the size and spectacle of it could rock anyone's resolve.

I was in that peculiar misery that follows as soon as you're handed what you ask for. Up close, it doesn't look quite the same.

On Lima Street, the garden was passing another peaceful night, still and quiet in a subtle glow. It was patient. It could wait forever for the gardener to return.

I wrestled with the question none of us can ever answer. How could I know for sure? Some things you can't fathom outright. Nothing is entirely what it appears to be; you might only see the half of it. You have to rely on a sliver of moonlight to get you through, because half of every day is night.

∽

I was headed down from a mountain retreat the first time I caught the chill wind of Maezumi Roshi's storied past. The topic came up while I was riding in a car bound for the airport with a group of fellow sojourners. I never saw it coming. It felt like the sudden plummet in temperature right after a winter sunset. First, I couldn't feel my fingers or toes. Then my nose went numb and my breathing stopped.

Maezumi was disgraced. He had been an inveterate lover of liquor and ladies, outted by a paramour and routed by his closest students ten years earlier. He had made a public confession and taken rebuke; made apology, done treatment; lost family and face; and placed the decision of whether he should stay or leave in the hands of his students. They voted for him to stay, and then most of them left.

Then I'd come along.

You might be wondering if I saw him differently after hearing the backseat gossip. I did see him differently. I saw him whole.

Learning the dark side of the saga shed light on things. Like why he practiced so devotedly and lived so humbly. Why he was so open and available, so weary, so kind. He was no less desperate than I. I was desperate to get something, and he was desperate to leave something behind. By anyone's standards, he was no saint. He was a poet. Everything about him was out in the open. Whether you could see the whole of it or not, he showed it all.

After my first retreat with him I was so grateful I offered him a favor I half-hoped he would ignore. I had seen the Zen Center's quarterly journal, which carried transcriptions of his talks. It looked like something I could do. "I am a writer," I said, flattering myself. "If you ever need any help with that sort of thing, let me know." He did need help, he said, and right away. What he had in mind was a book. He had never written one, although he lent his name to others' work. It wasn't that he was unproductive. In his midsixties and after more than forty years of practice, he felt too immature to contribute to the vast canon of Zen literature. Perhaps there was presentiment in his quick response that day, a hint of how little time remained.

"People will be drawn to you," he said, "and now you have something to share." I couldn't imagine what that might be.

Soon after, packages began arriving at my home. They contained cassette tapes of dozens of Maezumi's talks. Transcribing them was almost impossibly hard. Unschooled, I had no idea what I was listening to. I was dumb to the meaning and deaf to the language. To the casual listener, Maezumi might have seemed like the worst speaker in the world. In the middle of saying something, he would meander onto some other topic entirely and never return. There were sighs, pauses, punctuating laughs, shouts, and growls. He was not teaching in the conventional sense — giving explanations and instructions — he was talking to himself, reconciling dubious translations and expressing the ineffable substance of living truth. I couldn't make anything of it. When I admitted to him that I hardly understood a word of his, he laughed and said, "Put it in your own words!"

Sometimes I'd turn a tape over, expecting to hear the rest of a recording, and find it empty, the talk dead-ended. With all that working against me, the first transcription took me nearly a year of start-and-stop listening to produce in edited form. I gave the resulting document to Maezumi, and then I waited. He never spoke to me about it before he died. In the long silence I felt as if I'd failed him.

I'd transcribed his talks on a teaching by Dogen Zenji, the thirteenth-century monk and philosopher-king of Japanese Zen. Dogen's work was called "The Moon."

"Whether we see a crescent moon or a half moon, in any of the phases of the moon before it is full, is anything truly lacking?" Maezumi said in the talk. "Perhaps you are more logical than me," he laughed, "and you don't wait for the day your life will be full!"

One night a girl looked up at the sky through a veil of clouds and saw that half the moon was missing.

The moon is missing! The moon is missing! No one could convince her otherwise. In fact, she had seen it shrinking for some time, and every night came more proof of her worst fears.

I was right! This conviction was a pathetic consolation.

Where others might have seen a slice of shine, all she saw was the deepening hollow of absence.

There is something you think you don't have. A virtue, quality, or substance you think you need to acquire. Courage. Strength. Patience. Wisdom. Compassion. As soon as I name it, you see it as missing from you, quick to disavow the suggestion that you are complete.

I'm only human, you might say. I'm not at all whole and perfect. I'm injured, inadequate, and, yes, even a little bit robbed. Especially robbed.

She tried filling the hole with tears, shrieks, and bluster. She bought a toaster, a Sub-Zero, and a Maserati, a pile of shiny objects. They overflowed her house and storage unit. All of it made a mess, but nothing more. You can't fill a hole that doesn't exist.

And so, exhausted, she gave up and sat down, head heavy, heart leaden.

She didn't notice the shadows shifting into light, the wind lifting, the clouds parting, the days passing. One evening she opened her eyes and saw the moon. It was full, of course. It had been full all along, doing what moons do, reflecting light. Only our perspective changes. We rob ourselves when we mistake the unreal for the real.

Your heart is always whole, just as the moon is always full. Your life is always complete. You just don't see it that way.

"Just let everything and anything be so, *as it is*, without using any kind of standard by which we make ourselves satisfied, dissatisfied, happy, or unhappy. Then you'll see the plain and clear fact," Roshi told me on the recording. All that time I'd spent listening for the hidden meaning in his words, I hadn't heard even a word.

There is a pattern to it all. A precise and invisible orbit that brings the full moon around again without fail.

On seeing the garden, I recalled a night in 1994: the night before a New Year's Day, when I'd brought a new boyfriend — my future husband — to the Zen Center to meet Maezumi. We thought it was a terribly auspicious encounter, famous Zen master and all that, but Roshi had been lighthearted, joking about the little town east of LA where my friend lived, the town to which we'd one day return to make a life together. It was the eve of the year when everything would change: the year Maezumi would die, I would be married, and my life would take a slow but certain turn toward this ancient ground, not a glimmer of which was apparent at the time. Maezumi said something then that would guide me through this and every dark night after, the way moonlight penetrates shadow.

He said, "I was gardener there when I first came to America."

Later, a neighbor told us that the woman who had lived

here in the 1950s hired priests from the Zen temple to prune the pines. Maezumi had been here before; he'd shown me the Way. How could I waste another night of my life feeling lost and afraid?

When your eyes adjust to the moonlight, you can see exactly where you are. In the morning there would be work to do and a gardener to do it. I was following the footsteps straight on.

Part Two

LIVING NOW

Cover the ground where you stand.

CHAPTER 7

ROCKS
The Remains of Faith

One day Zengen, carrying a hoe, went up and down the hall as if searching for something. Sekiso said, "What are you doing?" Zengen said, "I am searching for the spiritual remains of our dead teacher."
— BLUE CLIFF RECORD, CASE 55

When you commit to a path, the Way opens up by itself.

A week after my return from California, as the house sale was pending, I had a call from an acquaintance. It was a long shot, but she knew someone who was looking to make a midlife leap. Was there any chance I'd be interested in getting rid of my business? The money wouldn't be much, but the buyer would take the furniture and keep the employees, and I'd be out of there in a hurry.

I had a complicated relationship with my job. The public relations business I'd started in my twenties was my baby, yes, but as I neared my forties I'd begun to think I'd brought the wrong baby home. I'd already sold it once, then taken it back, like any parent would, when I saw it faltering. It's hard to walk out a door that has your name on it, which seems like pretty solid evidence of who and what you are. But as with the gate in front of the garden, you have to pass through. The future beckons from the other side.

Next I heard from my landlord. I'd been renting a fixer-upper in the old Montrose neighborhood of Houston. He was sorry for the short notice, but he was starting a remodel and I would need to go.

In two months' time I was saying good-bye to the people and places I never thought I could live without. One of them was the *old me*. Movers took my small haul. I drove my sedan into the afternoon sun. Before I'd crossed the border into New Mexico, a stone shot out of the west Texas wasteland and cracked my windshield. Any lingering doubt was shattered. You are now leaving, the sign said. Don't look back.

Sometimes we feel a force beneath our feet, a tectonic glide atop the earth's convection, as if all we have to do is train our gaze straight ahead and be magically conveyed the rest of the way — kind of like the moving sidewalk at the airport, on a day it's actually working. We were in our new home by Independence Day. I was no longer the person I thought I was, doing the things I knew how to do. Sitting alone one weekday morning at the kitchen table, I cried long and hard. Then I went to the Rite-Aid and bought a wide-brimmed straw hat. Under the hat, all I had to go on was faith.

A carpet of ropey vines covered most of the ground in the garden. As if possessed of secret knowledge, I began pulling up vines with both fists. They lifted easily because they did not belong. An invader had stormed over a neighbor's fence during the garden's long neglect, wrapping itself around shriveled trunks and shrubs, creeping past the water's edge and dangling into the ponds like so many fishing lines. At first glance, the English ivy looked lush and even desirable, an opulent green glossing the surface of everything. But each yank revealed something smothered beneath, and the foundation of the garden began to emerge.

The backyard was the creation of a mysterious man named Tokutaro Kato, a landscaper whose name we found in old newspaper clippings and handouts from tours given half a century earlier. Reading the descriptions, we could reimagine parts of the garden that had long since disappeared — and what was probably sheer invention to begin with. Little was known of Kato. He was billed as an imperial gardener in Japan, but I doubted that bit of brag. I thought of him as a pilgrim roaming the California coast in the early 1900s looking for decent work and lodging among moneyed patrons. One story had it that he'd sat on this ground for three months before conceiving the garden plan. In Zen, a three-month period of sitting is called an *ango*, which means "peaceful dwelling." In matters of peace, you see, there can be no hurry.

What he conceived was a *stroll garden*, a common motif in Japanese landscape. A stroll garden is organized around three elements of nature — mountain, meadow, and ocean — encircled by stone paths. Walking the paths changes your perspective on a miniature world: from the base to the top of the mountain, through fields of shade and sun, from the near to distant shore, and around again and again.

Kato and his crew had dug enormous holes and moved tons of dirt. They quarried nearby canyons for hundreds of rocks and fit them into a granite hardscape of ponds and paths. The placement of the rocks into the pond banks was so precise that no mortar was visible between them. True, the mountain was now cloaked in vines, the meadow was choked in weeds, and the ocean was a stinking pit of sodden leaves. But the rocks stood exactly as they had been placed, guardians to the will and skill of the original gardener. Rocks formed this garden just as rocks formed the earth. Everything else was incidental. Everything else would fade away and be forgotten. It already had.

With time, even the existence of Kato was doubted, thought to be legend or lie. Scholars concluded there wasn't sufficient documentation to verify the authenticity of the garden or its maker. No solid evidence. They suggested the whole scheme might have been the handiwork of the property owner, a social-climbing suburbanite. Kato was written off.

One day I pulled up vines around the back of the mountain and found a flat stone laid in the earth, and then another and another, a clear path to the peak, hidden under a century of overgrowth. It was an archeological discovery that rivaled, for me, the treasure-laden tombs in Egypt's Valley of the Kings. *No solid evidence?* This was a rock that Kato had placed, in a spot where Kato had stood, giving a view he had bequeathed to *me*. Stones were his spiritual remains. Ground was the living proof. The rocks gave me faith.

I didn't need to know the garden's origin, because I knew the Way.

Clear the vines and find the rocks. Stand there and see for yourself.

⚭

Sundays in the summer I sat in a white wooden church in the middle of Thorndale, Texas, my mother's hometown. Inside the sanctuary it would be sweltering, the air humid and hellish by 10:00 AM, barely roused by the paper fans waving in every pew. These folk were my mother's kin, but I could not, for the life of me, see any resemblance to me. I was a normal kid, but the people around me seemed embalmed in age and hardship, barefaced and simple, relics from some old country no longer on the map. The organist would start in, and the wail from the flock was a keening dirge that rose from the dust of a failed sorghum crop, the grave of a stillborn baby, the memory of a soldier son who never came home. They held their hymnals with farmers' hands. Theirs was a climb from nowhere to nowhere with nothing to show for it. And yet they sang, and they knew the words.

On Christ the solid rock I stand.
All other ground is sinking sand.

Summers ended. All those people have since died. And I came out of my childhood believing that I was not like them — *no, not me* — that their place was not mine, that their faith was old-fashioned and foolish. I was wrong. Faith is a rock, an unavoidable rock, and one day you will fall to your knees at the sight of it.

Now and then folks will come to me and confess a secret. They're not really comfortable with my spiritual talk because they have no faith and don't know where to look for it. They are hobbled by dread, doubt, and fear. Because this is how they think, their lives seem to affirm it at every turn. They may be perpetually disappointed, terrified of the unknown, haunted by what-ifs. My heart breaks for them, but I don't believe their claims of faithlessness for one minute. It is impossible to live without faith. Having faith is as easy as inhaling oxygen and as reliable as gravity, the immutable laws of life. These laws are the solid evidence at the very bottom of Buddhism and are called dharma.

Dharma is never hard to find, but we are stubbornly blind to it, favoring, as we do, more inventive destinations.

Faith isn't something you can get from me. You can't get it from a book, not even a really good one. It isn't found in inspirational quotes, although it's nice to run across words of wisdom here and there. It's not something you get from a TV show or movie, not even a really uplifting one, because the good feeling fades as soon as the show is over. Faith isn't something you acquire when something really good happens or lose when disaster strikes. We say we lose our faith when bad things happen, but what we've lost is the false certainty, the comfortable bubble, that only good things happen to good people.

So where do you find faith? You won't believe me, but you already have it. You have it when you surrender to a night's slumber and open your eyes to another day. You have it every time you exhale, and in that half-second before you automatically inhale again. You have it when you put on your shoes, or when you don't, and walk across this planet without falling off the face of it.

Mine is not the faith of wishful thinking. It's faith with arms and legs, days and nights, eyes and ears.

The road you walk is an ancient one, on rocks placed long before you took your first step. No one knows how the world began or when it ends, where it comes from one minute or where it goes the next. Spiritual or scientific: one myth is as good as another. Either way you are unmistakably here, and that fact is no accident or imitation. Pull up the vines that hide the truth — your ideas and expectations; your doubts and foregone conclusions; your beliefs and fears, no matter how well-argued or self-righteous. Disentangle your feet. Take the path to the highest point and see the panoramic view of a place assembled without a plan. A place that's insufficiently documented. With no visible mortar or glue. Functioning with the perfection born of an intelligence you cannot comprehend.

Believe the rock. Believe the mountain, meadow, and ocean. Believe what you see right now.

That covers it.

Zen Mountain Center is located a mile high in the San Jacinto Mountains east of Los Angeles. This is where Maezumi Roshi planted his greatest faith. He aspired to create a major training center — an incubator — for the seeds of dharma in the West.

But it was untamed acreage, and the conversion of

rocky timberland into a *peaceful dwelling* would take more time, work, and money than one lifetime could muster.

"Little by little," Maezumi would say.

He brought in a geomancer to choose the most favorable locations for the Buddha hall and the zendo, and then he began to dig. The labor taxed blood and tears out of his students. They told stories of the endless excavations, the patience spent as Maezumi hauled and hoisted rocks into arrangements that were inexplicable to their tired eyes.

Each rock had a face, Maezumi said. He lifted and turned each rock until it faced forward. Until you could see it straight on.

Three months after meeting Maezumi, I traveled to a retreat on that mountain, where my morning work assignment was to clean a small rock garden that Maezumi had erected stone by stone. Sweeping fallen pine needles and leaves in a forest might strike some as pointless, but I took up the task as a test of spiritual attainment. I thought of myself as a quick study, and I was here to advance. I picked up each needle, each spine and speck of leaf, as if there was something to get. Something to prove.

Is this how? Is this right? Is this it?

He would walk by and smile at me as if he knew an inside joke.

There was nothing to get and nothing to prove. No higher authority, no validation, no prize. Clear your mind of the ivy that hides the face of things.

"Cover the ground where you stand," Maezumi said, and he meant the bare and unblemished ground of your life.

To see it, you'll have to uncover what's blinding you: the rampant rambling of your mind.

When something bad happens, when you step into the quicksand of your anxiety and doom, when your thoughts begin to race, when fear strangles your breath, despair wrenches your heart, and doubt suffocates the light right out of your day, pick up a rock and hold it in your hand. Yes, any old rock will do. Any rock will bring you back to the here and now. Faith in the here and now is faith that never leaves you. Besides, what else do you have to go on?

The couple that owned the garden before us had a child. Their child had a nanny, who said she twice saw a phantom standing in the garden in broad daylight. It was a man wearing black. Perhaps this was the spirit of the original gardener?

I had no doubt. Once I knew a man who wore black, and he'd told me to meet him right here.

CHAPTER 8

PONDS
The Right View

May we exist in muddy water with purity like the lotus.
— MEAL GATHA

We weren't doing the work all by ourselves. We had a yard guy.

The yard guy introduced us to a tree guy, and the tree guy suggested a sprinkler guy. The sprinkler guy knew a fertilizing guy whose brother-in-law was a fence guy. Before we did anything, though, we talked to a Japanese garden guy and asked him what we should do.

He said, "Spend twenty thousand dollars."

That wasn't going to happen. Not for a long while.

The cost of real estate in California can render anyone poor. We had been lucky to get in at the bottom of the market, buying the house for a little more than half of what it had sold for ten years earlier. But it was still a squeeze, and my prospects for work seemed slim. With twenty years of experience, I was overqualified for the few jobs out there and underqualified for the job right here.

This was upsetting. I thought I knew how to get things done, but I was at ground zero and already over my head. The roof needed replacing and the house needed to be repainted. There were creeping signs that the shower stall leaked. The air conditioner broke on a day when it was 115 degrees. I knew everything was old, but did it have to be *so old*? Neither was the garden quite what it looked like on that first innocent encounter. Junipers had been left to wither, their arms outstretched in rigor mortis. Aging azaleas had massed into a thicket of nearly bare branches. The pruning had been botched. The hardiest plants were ones that weren't supposed to be in a Japanese garden at all. Here and there were the errors of someone's misguided intentions — a Mexican palm, a pink rose bush, a baby apple tree — in our eyes, the offenses kept growing.

People gave us picture books about dreamy Japanese gardens, and we tormented ourselves with comparisons to the gems of Kyoto. My husband bought flats of delicate mosses at the nursery. He tried to coax them into our sandy topsoil. But the sun was too hot and the irrigation too uneven. It took two or three tries before we conceded. What was it exactly that made a garden Japanese? We decided it wasn't us.

Like the ocean to the earth, ponds covered three-fourths of the backyard. So we let the horticulture go for now and decided that what we really needed was a pond guy. The fish guy referred us.

We took him into the backyard and waited for the

diagnosis. He walked the circumference of the ponds, inspecting the waterfalls and the pump-activated stream that fed them. He stood back to get a sense of it all. He kneeled low to peer into the water. He put his hands on his hips and asked, "What did you say your problem was?"

We answered, "They're muddy."

Ponds are the heart of a Japanese garden, or so the literature told us. Kato shaped the four interconnected ponds into the form of the kanji character for *heart*, after the pond in an eighth-century temple garden in Kyoto. I wouldn't recognize a kanji character if it was tattooed on my ankle, let alone shaped out of a puddle on the ground. Looking at the ponds all day through my kitchen window, I couldn't see any semblance of it. Of course I understood that water really was the heart of things — the essence of life. At least on this plane of existence, water is life's source and sustenance.

The problem is what we put into it. Everything ended up in this water: leaves, seed pods, and branches from the messy sycamores; acorns and pollen from the oak; pine and cypress needles; redwood bark, bamboo leaves, palm fronds, spent blooms, mosquito larvae, tadpoles, turtles, bird feathers, fish poop, and virtually anything that could be loosened by the gusting easterly winds. (Everything can be loosened by the gusting winds in this part of California.) A family of raccoons romped in the water nightly, dining on frogs and koi and leaving parts behind. One morning the tables turned, and we had to fish a raccoon out of the pond. It had expired from some unknown cause in the night, a reminder of how little we knew about what was happening

under our noses. Traces of these — and other mystery in-
gredients — would stagnate, sink, and ferment into the thick
sediment at the bottom.

Our ponds were muddy. The water was an ugly brown,
laced with bright green strings of algae. It didn't look like
any koi pond we'd seen in a better homes magazine. We
thought it was sick, and that the few fish swimming in the
murk must be terribly sick too.

"This is the most perfect example of a naturally puri-
fied pond that I've ever seen," the guy finally said. He was
awestruck.

Then he showed us the hidden elegance in the whole rot-
ten mess. The large surface area supplied ample oxygen. The
stream and waterfalls were natural filters. The mud balanced
the water's chemistry, keeping plants and fish alive. The algae
was seasonal, triggered by temperature changes, and easy
to manage. The precise science of pond scum was beyond
my grasp, but the bottom line was this: ours wasn't like the
designer fish ponds decorating fancy homes and magazine
covers. This was the real deal. It would always be trouble —
ponds are a shitload of trouble — but it wasn't a problem.
Skim the leaves. Circulate the water down the stream and
falls. Let the mud settle, and the pond will purify itself.

He didn't do anything that day — except give us the right
view of the water. It isn't always pretty, but it's beautiful.

We never needed to call him again.

～

In Japanese there is a single word that means "heart, mind,
and spirit": *shin*. Japanese is not like English, in which we

divide into opposing concepts things that actually share the same indefinable essence. Like the ponds in my backyard: they look separate but are interconnected. Open the tap at the source, and the water from one pool swells into the other. Soon the illusion of separation disappears. The fish come to the surface and leap.

The word for a Zen retreat is *sesshin*, which means "unifying the mind." Ironically, Zen types argue about the meaning of the word, which is also defined as "gathering the mind" or "touching the mind." The differences don't matter. In the actual doing, the definitions of *sesshin* blend into one true thing: your life right here and now.

The mind we bring to a retreat is marvelous and fully functioning. As with water, the problem is what we put into it. The debris of old pain and resentments. The weight of grief and loneliness. The cloud of judgments. The poison of jealousy and anger. The anxious, internal rat-a-tat-tat pelting the present calm like a storm of stones. Buddha called these kinds of disturbances "upside-down thinking." By the time we come to *sesshin*, we feel as if we are drowning in a muddy flood, unable to breathe, see, or slow down. We can't imagine the deep stillness that lies beneath the waves.

A pond doctor enters the room with a reassuring smile and says, "You are a perfect example of natural purification." His medicine is nothing more than *zazen*, the way of sitting. He reminds you that you can inhale an infinite supply of oxygen without mechanical intervention. He tells you to follow the movement of your breath to clear distractions, and use your own senses to refresh your awareness. Naturally, disturbances occur, but you can right yourself again.

Sit still, just sit still and let the mud sink to the bottom. Your life rises up on a sturdy stalk and blooms on the surface like a lotus flower.

What goes into sitting isn't pretty, but after a while it becomes beautiful.

Now, what did you say your problem was?

❧

"I am not really living, I'm just existing." People say this to describe how lifeless they think their life is. But I'm sure their life is full of life. What they need is the right view.

Not long ago, while writing this chapter, I walked to the far perimeter of the garden opposite the house, following the path of stepping-stones placed at the original entry. This was the perspective intended for visitors to obtain on arrival. That's when I saw the shape of the ponds: clear as day, the kanji character *kokoro*, or heart. It had been there all along, but I been looking at it upside down.

In winter the ponds are beautiful. The wind has stopped. The sycamores are bare. I go to the trouble of scooping leaves out of the water, a job for life. (Nothing says Zen like shoveling pond scum.) The water lilies are dormant until spring. The fish are hiding in the mud until the last heron flies over. There is no movement beneath. The surface is a pristine mirror reflecting the empty trees and open sky. My heart is calm when I realize what all the gardeners before me had in mind for guests to see. They could wait for time and seasons to pass.

"I just wanted to sit together with people in this country," Maezumi said about his life's ambition. It sounds like so little, but modest ambitions can be the most heroic. In the years immediately following his scandal, Maezumi sat nearly alone. Sometimes only a handful of people would sit in the once-full zendo. If it happened to rain, even fewer would show up. Maezumi was not dissuaded. "Take care of the heart of the practice," he said to the few faithful. Then trouble is not a problem.

These days I want nothing more than to enter an empty room with a group of strangers and sit still and quiet in *samadhi*, nondistracted awareness, for the better part of a day. I am always astonished by the presence of people who would dare to do such a thing — burn perfectly good daylight to get nothing done.

To take responsibility for peace in your world is genuinely heroic. Practicing meditation can be hard on your stiff body and restless mind, but it does not hurt anyone. No one is harmed by your practice; indeed, everyone is helped. When you are still, no eyebrows are arched, no fists are clenched, no fingers are tapped, no sideways glances are given. When you are quiet, nothing mean, cruel, or critical is said.

We have the power to transform everything when we have the courage to do nothing. To make peace, stop tossing stuff into the water.

These days there is considerable discussion around the question, "What should Buddhism look like in the twenty-first century?" With neuroscience and technology at our disposal, the thinking goes, we should devise a practice that is more accessible than just old-style sitting, using means that are more relevant to modern life. I understand that people like things new and improved, tricked out, version 2.0, but this debate always confuses me. In my practice, there is no old way, there is no new way, there is just the Way. What is more modern than this moment? What is more accessible than breathing? What is more relevant than you? If you judge anything on the basis of how it looks, you will misjudge.

The beauty of a pond is that it is muddy.

This is my inexhaustible desire: that you will find a guide who is both patient and daring, unafraid to let you struggle, drift, and finally settle into the tempest of your own deep shit. One who will keep you quiet company as you go deep and dig until you look up and see that you are not sinking, you are not hopeless, your cause is not lost. There is no fix and no problem, no hurry and no wait. You are sitting upside up in the echoless calm of a vast, clear ocean, no wind or waves, and you are breathing, breathing, breathing.

CHAPTER 9

ROOTS
The Meaning of Life

A monk asked Joshu, "What is the meaning of Bodhidharma's coming to China?" Joshu said, "The oak tree in the garden."
— *THE GATELESS GATE*, CASE 37

From the beginning, I called it a grandfather tree, the oak tree in the garden. The reasons were self-evident. It was tall, broad-shouldered, and thick around the middle, like my grandfathers. Plus, I had an album of garden photos, handed down through generations, that showed the oak standing at full height before I was born. Only later did I learn that no such description exists in arboriculture. What I called a grandfather tree was instead *grandfathered*, protected from removal by a village tree ordinance. But that made sense too. It's impossible to remove your grandfathers from the line of life you've been given. When you're little, they hold you. You look up to them. They might teach you something useful that no one else has the time or patience

for. In time, they slow down, grow feeble, drop things —
but you can't do a damn thing about it.

Even approaching a hundred years old, the oak tree in
our garden was a fount of life. It cradled nests of marauding
rats and raccoons. Noisy squirrels chased the length of it all
day long. Jays shrieked, hawks roosted, and the wind flew
through its wide-open arms. Its canopy shaded a teahouse
built by a groundskeeper in the 1920s for his kids to play in.
That's a lot of hide-and-seek and games of tag: generations
of joy and laughter. Two years after we got here, our daughter, Georgia, was born. Suddenly, we saw only peril in a yard
full of rocks and water, not to mention *dirt*. If it had been left
to me, fear would have kept us locked indoors. But Georgia
kept proving that she was born to play in the garden, as we
are all born to play in the garden. She watched her step;
she knew her place. Before long, the neglected teahouse
was crawling with kids for parties and plays: revivals of *The
Wizard of Oz* and *Little House on the Prairie*, stories about
making yourself at home wherever you are, stories retold
with every generation.

The oak tree in the garden drops more than two thousand acorns a year. Each acorn is both a culmination and
a seed; each carries its own ancestral imprint and the full
potential to evolve. In California the principal propagator
of oaks is the scrub jay. A jay picks up thousands of acorns
and stores them underground in the fall, and when it's time
to eat, it remembers where nearly all of them are placed. A
few acorns stay undisturbed underground, and those are the
ones that sprout. The lineage of the coastal live oak depends
on what a bird forgets, and the survival of the Western scrub

jay depends on what a live oak leaves behind. It sounds like a willy-nilly proposition, but it isn't.

One acorn in ten thousand becomes a tree. On the one hand, what a waste. On the other, it works. In the crapshoot of life, you — *I mean you* — turned up. You rose from the ground of your ancestors, their dust in your bones. Without accomplishing another thing, you are the complete fulfillment of all those who came before you. How can you doubt yourself?

One summer, my grandfather in Texas taught me to whistle "Listen to the Mockingbird," a folk song wildly popular a century ago. All summer I studied my grandpa's mustached mouth and mimicked the sound that came out of it. When I started out, I got a hum. I got a spray of spit. I got a lot of empty air. I tried and tried, and then one day the pure notes rang out:

> Listen to the mockingbird,
> Listen to the mockingbird,
> The mockingbird still singing o'er her grave;
> Listen to the mockingbird,
> Listen to the mockingbird,
> Still singing where the weeping willows wave.

My grandfather was a gruff German American who didn't speak much English (at least that I could recognize), and I was only eight years old. I'm certain neither of us knew the lyrics until I put them on this page. What we shared was a wordless chirp, but now I see that we shared far more.

Inside this grandfather's house was a piece of furniture called a chifforobe, a musty wooden wardrobe with drawers. The very word was one of the secrets it contained, the strange double consonant like a vestige of lost meaning. To us kids, it was a toy chest.

The chifforobe stored a few fancy dresses worn to bygone dances and weddings by my mother and her sisters. On summer visits we granddaughters played pretend with them. But other things held my interest longer — old photographs of my phantom ancestors. I would flip through shoeboxes full of sepia images, staring into the stiff and grim faces of strangers. These people were Wends, a Slavic people who were part of an odd and oppressed sort of religious colony, which, like all colonies, no longer exists. Run out of Prussia in the late nineteenth century, they settled in the purgatory of central Texas. The Wends were serious about faith, hard work, and economy. The wedding portraits captured their high sobriety: the brides wore black to signify the life of toil awaiting them. This foresight was not in the least bit faulty.

These were my kin, somber in face and fashion, weighted by work and gravity, and much younger than they looked. The boys had jug ears and cowlicks. The girls wore ribbons. On the backs of some photos, salvaged from frames or torn from albums, were half-vanished names written in thin pencil. I pored over the faces, fascinated by the inconceivable fate that had brought me face-to-face with the departed. And then I would go outside and play under a chinaberry tree. That's where the action was. The action is always under a tree.

Trees figure prominently in wisdom teachings, perhaps because trees always figure prominently. Standing up by themselves, undisguised, bare to the bone, deeply rooted and yet reaching the sky, they show us the Way.

In one Zen story, a monk is planting trees around the monastery. It's grimy, back-breaking work, but he doesn't quit. The teacher asks him, "Why are you planting so many trees right here in this deep valley?" The monk isn't wasting his life on imponderables. He replies, "First, to improve the scenery." He's cultivating the Way. Everything looks better with a little work. "Second, to serve as a guide for those who come after." So we have trees to teach us now.

Buddha himself was awakened while sitting under what is called the bodhi tree, which means "enlightenment tree." The exact species was a *Ficus religiosa*, a sacred fig tree native to India. Any tree would have done the trick. How many trees have you passed by already today while lost in a daydream? Buried in thought?

The story of Buddha's enlightenment goes like this. Tired of the same kind of search you're on, he sat down under a tree, and he didn't get up. He sat there, night and day, until he found the meaning of life. In the early hours of the eighth day he looked up and saw the morning star in the east, Venus bathed in sunlight, foretelling the imminent dawn on earth. You can see it nearly any morning if you wake up in time. He said, "I, the great earth, and all beings simultaneously attain the Way!" It was an expression of awe and astonishment. What if you suddenly saw through all your fear and ignorance, your restless craziness, and realized that you already possess what you are looking for because you already *are* everything you are looking for? The Buddha didn't see something invisible. He saw something he'd missed all his life: all of life. Rising up from the deep beneath, covering the earth, reaching the sky, containing every speck of everything and everyone through all space and time.

This is the secret your grandfather leaves behind — the most intimate secret of life. You.

You are born.

Let's consider the facts before we get carried away.

You are born, and no one — neither doctor, scientist, priest, nor philosopher — knows where you came from. The whole world, and your mother within it, was remade by the mystery of your conception. Her body, mind, and heart were multiplied by a magical algorithm whereby two beings come together as one and one being becomes two.

You inhale and open your eyes. Now you are awake.

By your birth, you have attained the unsurpassable. You have extinguished the fear and pain of the past, transcended time, turned darkness into light, embodied infinite karma, and carried forth the seed of consciousness that creates an entire universe. All in a single moment.

You are your grandfather's hope and your grandmother's heart. You are the living evidence of a beginningless beginning. Don't bother with the how, why, or when.

Now that you are here, you manifest the absolute truth

of existence. You are empty and impermanent, changing continuously, turning by tiny degrees the wheel of an endless cycle. Just a month from now, your family will marvel at the growing heft of your body. They will delight in the dawn of your awareness. You will grab a finger and hold tight, turn your head, pucker your lips, and eat like there's no tomorrow. You will smile. Six months from now, the newborn will be gone. Within a year or so, you will be walking the earth as your dominion. And although your caregivers might think that they taught you to eat, walk, and talk, these attributes emerged intuitively from your deep intelligence.

You are born completely endowed with the perfected wisdom of the awakened mind. You are a miracle. You are a genius. You eat when hungry and sleep when tired. You are a buddha. But in the same way that you will forget the circumstances of your birth, you will forget the truth of your being. And by forgetting what you are, you will suffer in the painful, fruitless search to become something else, striving against your own perfection to feel whole and secure. By your attachment to desires, you will squander the chance of endless lifetimes: the chance to be born in human form. Luckily, the chance to be reborn — to wake up — arises every moment. Your body is the body of inexhaustible wisdom. When will you realize it?

If you don't believe it, have a baby. Or simply notice in each instant that you are giving life to a world that is brand-new. Mothers face fear, sickness, and pain to be handed a crowning glory: the opportunity to bring a new life home and leave an old life behind. We are each, no matter what, given this gift right now.

To be sure, birth is not apart from death, not its opposite, not its foe, but synchronous with it: one thing.

In each moment of birth, we lose what we no longer need: the beliefs of who and what we are and what we can and can't do. We learn that life is not ours alone but shared through all space and time, not defined by what we like, want, know, or think. We get a good look at how much trouble we cause; how stubborn, selfish, and terrified we are; and how much growing up we still have to do.

We learn the true nature of love as effortless and abiding, flowing naturally and forgiving everything. This love is compassion, and it is born when we are no longer deceived by appearances: the illusion that "I" exist separate from "you," the "you" that I blame when I am selfish, embittered, and angry. Compassion is the fearless essence of life. It endures, enhances, and sustains itself. It is generous and good. It drops two thousand acorns every year from a single oak. Perhaps one of them will hit you on the head or pierce the tender sole of your bare foot, occasioning yet another breakthrough.

As a parent, I have learned that I have limitless love to give, and I can start by loving myself. I can love, trust, and care for my own body. I can illuminate my own mind and open my own heart. I can change habits, practice discipline, overcome fears, and quiet my criticism. I can be generous. I can give myself away. Above all, I can keep from harming my child and anyone's child. After all, we are the children of one another, interconnected and interdependent. By our practice, we learn to parent ourselves and care for everyone.

The facts of life keep reappearing even while we are carried away by blind fear and distraction. So here is another chance.

You are born. You inhale and open your eyes. Now, are you awake?

He says he has been waiting for someone like me, someone with a capacity to learn, someone who understands the heart of the dharma. At that moment, I have no earthly idea what he's talking about. I'm pretty sure this isn't the first time he's said something like this. He could have said it to everyone; teachers say the same thing over and over, praying that something sinks in. An oak drops hundreds of thousands of acorns in a lifetime. Percentage-wise, nothing much comes out of it.

But I listened, and later that day, I wrote the words down on the back of a creased sheet of paper printed with my first *sesshin* instructions. I'm holding that paper in front of me right now. Sitting undisturbed in my desk drawer for twenty years, the words took root in me. Roots feed by osmosis, the slow absorption of nearby nutrients.

Life is transmitted with nearly impossible and inexplicable precision, and Zen teaching accords with nature. We are each the fruit of ancestral seeds — thoughts, words, and actions — that reveal their own meaning through us. Like it or not, we each carry the indelible marks of our lineage. In the same way that we have a physical lineage, we have a spiritual one, although you may not yet realize yours. In the same way that trees derive their life from the soil, they take it from the sun as well. Anything and everything that comes to us comes through a lineage, because that's how life works: by cause and effect.

Lineage is not a choice of this or that. In lineage, as in life, you get what you get.

It's quite plain to see. My eyes are my mother's. My nose is my dad's. I whistle like a mockingbird. I come from a long line of the patient and persistent. I am the heir of their dreams and disappointments, the salt in their tears. I came out of the chifforobe, and I will yet join the ranks of its unremembered. But that's not the end of it. What we do with our one life makes a difference for all time.

Ten years after beginning my practice, I ordained as a priest. Now I am a woman wearing black. I belong to a Zen lineage that spans eighty-one generations of ancestors, each of whom transmitted the teaching one-on-one, face-to-face, to his or her successors. This is nothing I sought. I simply arrived in the place where I already stood to receive what was already in my hands. What kind of a student would I be if I didn't honor my place in line or repeat the refrain I've been given? And so I bequeath the same to you. "Doubts do not grow branches and leaves," an old ancestor said seven hundred years ago. Let's see what you do with your arms and legs; with your breath, sweat, and blood. It's an awesome responsibility to inherit the ground where you stand.

Maezumi was famous for saying simply, "Appreciate your life." He didn't mean conjure up a sentiment of gratitude or abundance. He didn't mean make a bucket list or count your blessings. He meant *don't* conjure, list, or count!

Appreciate your life by waking up. When you wake up, the meaning of life comes to life through you.

On the day you were born, the grass danced and the air sang. The sun rose up and bowed beneath the moon's mystery. The stars harmonized in silent symphony. The ocean lulled the earth beneath a foggy vest, making a rich and ready nest. Your mother and father, every mother and father, came together and apart, entrusting their lives to you, making a place for you to come home. People ask me if my daughter has ever read anything I've written about her. Oh, yes, she's read all sorts of things that were shortsighted or insensitive, things I'd rather she forgot. If you should ever encounter her, do as my grandfathers before me, and point her toward the gift that is already hers, the gift that is already yours: the oak tree in the garden.

CHAPTER 10

BAMBOO
A Forest of Emptiness

Avalokitesvara Bodhisattva, doing deep prajna paramita,
Clearly saw emptiness of all the five conditions,
Thus completely relieving misfortune and pain.
— HEART SUTRA

It floats like a curtain between chaos and calm, veiling the way to paradise. Once beyond the barrier, there is no turning back.

Even its names are seductive: Chinese Goddess, Golden Fishpole, Himalayan Blue, Fountain, Sweet Dragon, Moonlight, and Wine. In the breeze, it whispers. In a tempest, it groans. All legs and slender tendrils, fanning long fingers: it is nature's exotic dancer. From the get-go, we were entranced.

You can fall in love with bamboo, but be careful which one you choose, or you could be trapped in your own attachment. The wrong one in the wrong place will overrun your premises, exploit your weaknesses, corrupt your foundation, topple fences, and collapse your roof. And that's in the first year of your relationship.

There are more than a thousand varieties of bamboo. We did the research when we realized we were surrounded on all sides and losing ground. Bamboo falls into two categories: Clumping bamboo grows slowly on short roots in one place, like the giant bamboo at our front gate. This is the nice and easy kind. Well behaved, it won't give you any trouble and will lull you into thinking you are safe. Running bamboo spreads across the porous borders of your defenselessness. It is nothing short of a global disaster.

Bamboo had lately come into widespread use as an earth-friendly building material, and based on our experience, we began to view its attributes with a jaded eye.

It's durable. *You can't kill it.*

It's sustainable. *It always grows back.*

It's a grass. *It's a weed.*

It's one of the fastest-growing plants on earth. *It will mow you down.*

It's flexible. *You can't break it.*

It works as a screen. *You can't get beyond it.*

It's stronger than steel. *Tell me about it.*

Running bamboo will erupt into your bed of roses, infiltrate the fruit trees, and nose through the cracks of your front porch. It grows under asphalt, through concrete, and in the invisible gaps between mortar and brick. What you once desired, you will soon despise. Think I'm exaggerating? Dozens of communities have banned running bamboo as a menace to peace and property. A war of man versus nature has spread to neighbors versus neighbors, with no end in sight.

My husband devoted weekends to excavating the front yard, digging up invasive bamboo roots, or rhizomes, that lie just under the turf like landmines. Running bamboo sends out lateral roots vast distances from the parent plant. It's hard to map its source or trajectory. To contain it, experts nonchalantly advise you to plant runners behind three-foot-deep underground barriers like nuclear bunkers. Not even that works. We cursed the guy who dropped a payload of Golden Fishpole on this site fifty years ago. If he weren't already dead, we would have strangled him.

Late one night when the Santa Ana winds raked the mountain canyons at fifty miles an hour (which is not altogether uncommon), the bamboo shimmied and moaned for hours. Awake in the storm, we heard a thundering boom over our heads. A colossal stand had given way, busting through a rock-walled planter and bringing a twenty-foot section of our neighbor's fence with it. The stalks thudded onto the roof over our heads. Pulled aboveground by the fall, the root mass was as dense as granite and weighed a ton. Like single blades of grass, bamboo stalks have no independent existence. They rise from a common root system, and that root system is *big*. It took five men two days to carve it up and carry it off. Our roof had held, luckily, but our resolve was broken. We'd seen into the belly of the beast. This was a war we couldn't win with hand shovels and shears. There was only one way to bring the battle to an end, the way to bring all battles to an end.

To make peace, stop fighting. In the struggle between

you and your world, sign a permanent ceasefire. Let bamboo be bamboo. You sure as hell can't turn it into anything else. When the smoke clears, you're going to see that your enemy isn't what he appears to be.

Under the sheath of its skin, bamboo is empty. Absolutely everything is.

∽

Form is emptiness and emptiness is form. This single phrase is the summation of the Buddhist path, the culminating insight of the Way. But having uttered it, I've already strayed from it. Having read it, you've missed it, because now your mind is running amok trying to understand it, and here I am trying to chase after you. So let's come back together in one big, empty space and start over.

What looks solid is not solid; what has no shape comes in all shapes. In a physical sense, bamboo is strong because it is hollow. It is supple and resilient; it bends without breaking. It supports incredible weight. It grows unimpeded by any known barrier, spreading outward everywhere. This is true of you too. Where do you think you begin and end? At your feet? Your head? Your skin? Your eyes, nose, mouth, ears? Your thoughts, memory, feelings? The way we limit ourselves imposes a bunker mentality and defies reality.

We experience our lives through the senses, a truly marvelous thing. In the split second after the pure cognition of seeing, hearing, smelling, tasting, touching, and thinking, we form a reaction to a sense object: attraction or aversion, liking or disliking, the subjective judgment of good or bad. What you might dispassionately call *Phyllostachys aurea*,

Golden Bamboo, I see as Public Enemy Number One. No matter how we react to our environment, the environment has no gripe with us. Every war is a war with ourselves. Everything is empty and ephemeral. We can turn anything into a weapon to wreak havoc and destroy peace, and we do. Human beings fight hundred-year wars.

If you doubt any of this, remember what you took on faith in fourth-grade science. All matter is composed of atoms. Atoms are empty space. By definition you can't see emptiness. You can't even imagine it. But you can be it. You already *are* it. Now, to live and let live in emptiness: that's the secret to paradise. It's a secret hidden in plain sight, but it can take you forever to crack the code.

First, be quiet. Give away your ideas, self-certainty, judgments, and opinions. Drop your personal agenda. Let go of defenses and offenses. Face your critics. They will always outnumber you.

Lose all wars. All wars are lost to begin with. Abandon your authority and entitlements. Release your self-image: status, power, whatever you think gives you clout. It doesn't, not really. That's a lie you've never believed.

Give up your seat. Be what you are: unguarded, unprepared, and surrounded on all sides. Alone, you are a victim of no one and nothing.

You are as ready as you'll ever be; you were born ready. The possibilities are endless. Reject nothing.

What appears in front of you is your liberation — that is, unless you judge it. Then you imprison yourself again.

Now that you are free, see where you are. Observe what

is needed. Do good quietly. If it's not done quietly, it's not good. Start over. Always start over.

Even now, as you read along, are you formulating an objection to this in your mind? Because that's what I do, and that's what I have to stop — the endless, imaginary debates, the pros and cons of this and that. They wear me out.

Nowadays I spend most of my time sitting in a chair and pounding into a keyboard. It's long and silent work, and I lose myself in it, but I know where to go for a kick of adrenaline. I click over to a social media site, where I'll find a new skirmish gathering speed, inciting the community's opinion, anger, and rebuke. I understand why we do that — I too can be self-righteous — but I am battle fatigued. The world cries for compassion. It craves acceptance and belonging. It needs our attention, a kind word, a smile, a wave, a handshake, or a hug. Are we against *everything*? Angry at *everyone*? Sometimes it seems the only thing we'll speak up for is a fight.

I push back from the fray and step out into the garden where the leaves rustle and bend in gentle rhythm with the wind. The air is fresh. The sky is blue. It's an amazing place we live in when we're not at odds with it. Who can contain the love that this one life brings with it? It is boundless.

On the street outside the gate, a woman walks a dog. I've glimpsed them nearly every day for what must be years. Her dog is old and the woman goes slowly, the two now inseparable on the steepest part of the hill.

"It's a beautiful day," I say.

"It sure is."

Someone once asked Maezumi Roshi why he practiced. "To make my heart tender."

❧

We were sitting around the room with our backs to the walls, empty space in the center. This time we were not facing away from one another in *zazen*, but rather toward each other, for the purpose of sharing.

A group of practitioners had asked Maezumi to convene a meeting because some of them weren't getting along. They were bothered by the way things were going. Other people were taking liberties, exploiting their status, not doing their share. It wasn't right; it was unfair. They wanted Maezumi to hear them out so he could intervene and discipline the offenders. It always helps, they said, to bring an upset out into the open so something can be done about it.

I was a visitor, so I said nothing. My practice was hard enough to maintain just by myself. No one else was making it harder. But as an impartial observer, I could see where the problems originated.

Everyone said his or her piece. Arrows flew through the room. Maezumi heard it all and seemed genuinely bewildered. He was quiet for a long time.

We come together to practice like trees in a forest, he said. No tree bothers any other. Every tree shares the same ground, light, water, food, and space. Each grows according to its own capacity and the conditions present. Trees grow upright and strong, and together create a place of shelter and beauty. Where exactly is the problem?

Human relationships are not that simple, someone countered, exasperated at the old man's cultural blindness. These days people require a more sophisticated approach — taking into account personal histories, biases, and feelings — don't you think?

"Don't think," he said.

Many left the room unsatisfied. As for the teacher, he looked tired.

"As we practice together sincerely, we become increasingly aware that internal and external cannot be separated. This is the growing awareness of the real harmony that underlies everything." That's what Maezumi tried to bring to life in his teaching. Some folks will fight harmony to the death.

I can't tell you when the bamboo was no longer the bane of our existence. Somewhere along the way it turned back into bamboo. For one thing, shovels really do make a dent. Even modest effort pays off in the long run. Nothing is the hindrance we make it out to be.

Once we had our own little sprout, our hands were full just trying to keep up with her growth spurts. When she got a little older, we needed to add a bedroom onto the house. The builder brought in a bulldozer to dig up the front yard and haul off the displaced sod. With that, the roots of our outrage seemed to disappear. Inside and outside, everything has come together quite nicely.

Shoots still crop up in the darnedest places. If they bother me, I take care of them. Sometimes, they come back and I take care of them again. My practice is taking care of things. Besides, how can I object? Now and forever, this is the Way to paradise.

CHAPTER II

PALM
The Eternal Now

Let me respectfully remind you,
Life and death are of supreme importance.
Time swiftly passes by and opportunity is lost.
Each of us should strive to awaken. Awaken!
Take heed. Do not squander your life.

— EVENING GATHA

There is a time machine in my backyard. It transports travelers three hundred million years into the past and three hundred million years into the future. For the time being, it is a kind of short, sturdy palm that proliferates on our property, a living fossil from the age of dinosaurs. Its kinfolk populate deserts and rainforests, survive in sand and swamps, and flourish either in sun or shade. The trunk has no lateral branches, rising straight up from a taproot. Born from a seed with a solitary leaf, it turns over a new leaf once a year. At first, its changes are almost imperceptible. As it ages, the pace quickens. Seemingly overnight, a crown of new leaves unfurls all at once, encircling its head. Splayed open like this, it lives more than a hundred or maybe even a thousand years, outlasting anyone's count.

If you want a glimpse of the past or future, take a look at it now. Presently, it isn't going anywhere.

The lineage is ancient, but modern species are relative newborns, arriving on the scene twelve million years ago, a blink in geologic time. Believed to be near extinction, the plants are harvested for sale to collectors and illicitly traded by thieves. Conservation efforts have been unsuccessful.

The *Cycas revoluta*, or Sago palm, is named for the shape of its baby leaflets, which curl along their spine like the revolution of a circle. The Sago is not really a palm, nor is it a fern or a conifer, each of which it resembles. It is a shape-shifter from an alternate universe, an ambassador from infinity. It is time itself, and time itself is timeless.

A cycad's characteristics will give you a lot to chew on, but don't. The plant is poisonous and can bring on paralysis. The seed is toxic and causes dementia. Its stems are barbed, and its leaf tips razor sharp. Pay attention, or you'll regret it.

Our cycads were original to the garden, but we didn't fully appreciate them at first. For one thing, we didn't like the way they looked. They aren't exactly pretty. Durability isn't soft on the eyes. Rare in some parts of the world, cycads were multiplying all over ours. Once we learned how valuable they were, we tried to profit from our windfall, prying off the "pups," or offspring, and trading them for pricey exotics at the nursery. But none of the dainties lasted. Precious things disappear in an instant, while the same old thing seems to hang around forever.

What are you to make of something that you don't like the looks of; that is both highly prized and commonplace, imperceptible and everywhere; that makes you wince with pain; and that in the end, is going to kill you? What will you make of time? The best use of time is to transcend it, and since your life depends on it, there isn't time to waste.

Got a minute? For this, yes, you really do.

The essential business of Buddhism is time. You might think the business of Buddhism is wisdom and compassion, serenity, nirvana, peace, harmony, and such, but you can't arrive at any of that without altering your view of time. It's worth your time, because seeing into the true nature of time is seeing into the true nature of you.

There's an old story about a young monk who encountered an old monk toiling in the midday heat. This wasn't a halfhearted young monk; this was a sincere one who had made a long trip, hoping to arrive at a deeper understanding of life. The old guy was the monastery cook, looking pained and bent, spreading mushrooms out to dry in the scorching afternoon sun. He had chosen a miserable time to do it, and had not even put on a hat. The young monk felt sorry for him, and maybe guilty that the fool was suffering so much to prepare food for a horde more able-bodied than he. Perhaps it would be wise, even kind, to suggest a different way.

"Why don't you have a helper do this?"

"Others are not me."

"The sun is so hot and you're working so hard. Why don't you do it another time?"

"Until when should I wait?"

At that, the young monk shut up. The old coot wasn't suffering. He was completely absorbed in the moment.

Even though we might feel so busy all the time, without a minute to stop, we hesitate in all kinds of ways. With fear: "I can't do it." With doubt: "There's no way." With judgment: "I don't like this." With resentment: "Not fair!" With anger: "%&*$##@" With avoidance: "Not now." With blame: "It's your fault." With arrogance: "It's not worth my time." With selfishness: "Let someone else do it." I could go on and on, and the problem is, I do. The work of ego is to resist, and ego works around the clock if you let it.

The ignorance of infinite lifetimes comes to a sudden halt the moment you stop thinking that there is some other person, some other day, some other where, and some other way. It's like turning over a new leaf. Dogen Zenji, the young monk in this story, called Zen "the wholehearted Way" — engaging in your everyday activities with nothing left over and nothing left out. When you apply the Way to everything you do, your life becomes your practice. You see that time is not apart from you, is not your enemy or captor; time *is* you.

I recall this story whenever I hear someone say she is trying to live in the now. We typically say this with our heads tucked in humility, as if confessing a secret aspiration for which we believe we lack the talent, opportunity, and training. *Someday I'm going to star on Broadway. Go to the moon. Live in the now.* But we are all living in the now. Now is the only time there is. Right now, you might think you are living in the past or future, but you are only *thinking* about another time. Nostalgia seems like a harmless pastime until it renders you blind. Worry seems like a reasonable activity until it renders you insane. When our thoughts dwell in a neverland, we're bound to feel sad, angry, afraid, power-less, inadequate, or overwhelmed. If you feel that way, it's a good bet that you've gotten ahead or behind the times. Per-haps it would be kind, even wise, to suggest a different way.

Someday must be the great lie of our lifetimes. We tell it for forty or fifty years. After that, we trade its false promise for the dead sentiment of the *good old days*. Both are thieves that will steal time right out from under your nose, and you will grieve your passing life as if robbed.

Someday, I told myself, I was going to sit a long retreat. This was in the good old days. I signed up for ten days, but by the second day I wanted out. Midway through the sleepy dawn sitting, I slunk out of the meditation hall into what I thought would be the invisibility of my dorm room. I didn't plan to stay away long. I would just take a short break from the aching effort of staying awake. I was a beginner, you know, doing my best, and I thought I deserved a little *me* time. It would be a while before I began to realize that, no matter what I'm doing, it's *all* me time. A few minutes into my escape, the door opened and two staff members came in and convened an impromptu meeting right next to me as I lay mortified on my foam mattress, staring up at the ceil-ing. That woke me up! I couldn't wait to get out of my get-ting out.

At no time during the next twenty years of practice have I ever fled a sitting period, although I've wanted to. Of course, there are many ways to flee discomfort and dif-ficulty, and I've explored just about all of them unsuccess-fully. The best place to practice is a place you don't want to be, using the time you don't think you have.

That morning I learned that resolving the great matter of life and death starts with the little matter of showing up. I showed up to the zendo every morning, every afternoon, and every evening. I showed up to sit in one spot, upright, and watched the light rise and fall overhead. I surrendered; I settled; I entered *samadhi,* which means I stopped running around in my head. As much. The time that followed wasn't fast or slow. It wasn't long or short. It didn't come or go. When the retreat was over, I went home happy and excited, babbling about the discovery I had made.

"I know what a day is!" I said to my roommate at the time. He suspected I'd been off chasing unicorns and rainbows. "It is daylight, followed by darkness, followed by daylight!" He looked at me funny. Maybe these retreats weren't such a good idea. I made no sense, but I was trying to describe what I'd seen: a day has no beginning and no end. It goes on forever. Conditions change, that's for sure. The light shifts and the breeze moves; the temperature goes up and down; people are born and they die; the pages on a calendar flip; the second hand sweeps; toenails grow and hair falls out; but time itself stands still. There is no greater joy than seeing through time, because then you've touched the leaf tip of eternity, which looks exactly like your backyard right now, overgrown with time.

Where else could eternity be but right here now?

∾

One day a dinosaur stomped on a sturdy palm and sent the seeds shooting three hundred million years in all directions.

I can't see how, but I can see *now*. A single moment of reality is all you ever need to see it all.

Maezumi Roshi used to follow nearly everything he said with a question: "See?" You might assume he meant, Do you understand? But now I know he didn't. You have to stop trying to understand before you can really see things as they are, see yourself as you are.

"We should thoroughly study ourselves from top to bottom. Our existence has nothing to do with the old or new, the past or the future. The time we are living right now exists *as it is*. There is no way to compare it to anything else. It is more than enough. It is the life of the sun and the moon, the life of the mountains and the rivers, the life of hundreds of grasses and myriad forms. See?" This is something Maezumi said. See?

But we don't see, and so we pass our time blind to time.

It's relatively easy to see the changing aspect of time — what comes and goes — and hard to see the unchanging aspect — what never leaves. Yet both sides exist in a single moment. The superficial ups and downs bring us laughter and tears, excitement and boredom, joy and terror. But beneath the changing appearances, our awareness is still and steady. Awareness is our salvation: where we find spiritual security, faith, and fearlessness. Our own awareness enables us to love truly and deeply instead of clinging vainly to what passes by. It allows us to live knowing that we will grow old, get sick, and die.

It's one thing to watch other people die, thinking all the while that it's not your time. But it's always your time.

Before the lights go out in a monastery, a monitor breaks the silence of the hall with a piercing admonition:

> Let me respectfully remind you,
> Life and death are of supreme importance.
> Time swiftly passes by and opportunity is lost.
> Each of us should strive to awaken. Awaken!
> Take heed. Do not squander your life.

And we're supposed to sleep on that.

This is still the age of dinosaurs, only these days I'm the dinosaur. I am now fifty-seven years old, and the changes are happening fast. Durability isn't soft on the eyes. My hair has grayed enough for me to be called gray haired. With my magnifiers, I can see that some of the freckles on my face are really liver spots, and the wrinkles are not just laugh lines. Life's major milestones — those birthdays we call the "big ones" — have slipped past my reliable recollection. I am at an age when I am irritating to a precious few and invisible to everyone else. All these changes are as plain as day, but even so, I don't know where the time went.

Some nights as I put myself to bed, a tremor comes over me with the thought that *there's no time*. Of course there's no time, but what I mean is that in my house there is no baby, no little girl, no tween, no new bride, no young mother, no thirties, no forties, no fifties, no yesterday, no tomorrow, and no someday. This is real, people! There is no time to question how much or little time there might be, where to go or when, what comes after, how to end up, the next great thing I should or could do. The days of wondering are spent.

Overnight, my daughter has grown up and I have grown old. Everything came too late, went too fast, and now it's gone too soon! My heart seizes in grief. My body clenches in fear. I am powerless and paralyzed.

Now, how will I get out of this one?

There's only one way. As I breathe, my mind and body relax. My palms unfurl. Worry lifts, and I drift into the darkness one more time. Eternity rests right here.

CHAPTER 12

....

PINE
A Disappearing Breed

This birth and death is the life of buddha.
— DOGEN ZENJI

There were parts of the garden we couldn't kill if we tried. That was our saving grace. But from the beginning, the pines seemed too far gone.

A masterfully pruned pine is the pinnacle of a Japanese garden, the measure of its success. Three pines leaned over the rim of our ponds as if poised on the brink of an abyss. They were stunted, their branches twisted, some withered and bare. Dead needles clung to them like rust. No matter how they looked now, we knew they had once been tended carefully. They bore the faded marks of a long-forgotten art.

In the garden, pines symbolize endurance, the capacity to withstand harsh realities. They are sometimes pruned the way a coastal wind can strip a cliffside pine: to within an inch of its life, which looks like an inch of its death. On this balancing point they are appreciated in full.

Ours were tipping toward extinction.

We asked a fellow from the nearby county arboretum to come take a look. He said we were killing them with too much water in some places and too little water in others. The trunks were soaked and the roots were starved. Top-heavy overgrowth blocked sunlight from reaching spindly under-growth. They needed to be thinned and shaped, revived with a surgeon's practiced touch.

We were as likely to slice into the pines as we were to perform our own appendectomies. We went looking for a hero.

It took us eleven years to find Mr. Isobe.

Japanese gardeners are a disappearing breed, at least in California, where upward mobility and age has natu-rally diminished the ranks. The first Japanese immigrants in Southern California were not imperial gardeners; they were farmers, forbidden by law to own or lease land. They worked as farmhands until they could acquire plots in the names of their American-born children. Japanese American farmers eventually produced just under half of all vegeta-bles grown in the state, including nearly all tomatoes, straw-berries, celery, and peppers. Their futures were upended by forced internment in relocation camps during the Second World War. Dispossessed of their property and jobs, they were released at war's end into an underclass. With garden-ing as a handhold, they returned to life.

At one time, an estimated one in four Japanese American

men worked as gardeners. These men did not pass on their trade to their offspring; they wanted education and advancement for their children. Over the next fifty years, the Japanese gardening community shriveled to the size it is now, with fewer than one hundred gardeners still at work around Los Angeles. If you lived as a Japanese gardener, you probably died as a Japanese gardener, and the pine trees went with you.

It took us eleven years to find Mr. Isobe, and only four more to lose him again. That's how it goes with the great ones.

⁊⁊

What do you call the kind of world where your job vanishes, your marriage dissolves, your baby grows up, cancer spreads, hearts stop, your parents die, buildings collapse, your pension tanks, your hip gives out, the milk goes bad, and a new car loses 20 percent of its value just by being driven off the lot? You call it the Way.

The nature of life is impermanence. One day it'll get your attention. Reality might dawn in a single blow or accumulate in a thousand cuts, but one way or another you'll see that things change. Nothing is solid. Everything disappears. In a million, billion ways the world will fail you. How can you bear it?

The greatest Japanese Zen master was Dogen Zenji. Scholars trace the birth of his spiritual quest to his mother's death in 1207 when he was seven. At her funeral, he saw the smoke from an incense stick rise up and disappear into thin air. Thereafter, he was unsatisfied with half-truths about life and death. He entered a monastery as a boy but was unconvinced by what he heard there and began to doubt that anyone could resolve his questions about the Way. He traveled to China when he was twenty-three to study in the old style, with masters of Chan, the forerunner of Japanese Zen. There, an elderly teacher cut through his confusion with one clean stroke, saying, "To study Zen is to drop off body and mind."

Soon after, his teacher died and Dogen returned to Japan. He founded the Soto school of Zen and devoted his life to teaching and writing, producing a mountain of essays, practice instructions, letters, and poems — the work of a genius. His teaching was emphatic and uncompromising, original and provocative. Given the political chaos and religious warfare of the time, he was not widely patronized or even well liked. He died when he was only fifty-three years old, whereupon his work was ignored for five hundred years.

Maezumi Roshi might have been Dogen's biggest fan. He devoted his life to the study and clarification of Dogen's teaching. It didn't matter if no one listened or cared. He took up Dogen almost every time he gave a talk, delving into the deep reaches of the old man's mind — while students stifled groans or nodded off — touching a brilliance that few could even imagine. He said that Dogen was the birth and death of Japanese Zen, the beginning and end. Nothing came before and nothing after. What about Maezumi, didn't he matter? He frowned. "I'm an American."

◦⁀◦

Mr. Isobe called himself Jeffery, although his birth name was Nobuaki, a samurai name. He wore a long-sleeved shirt buttoned to the collar, belted khakis, and a straw hat. A crew came with him, two industrious helpers ready to mow and blow, but we told him to focus on the foliage when he came once a week. We wanted him to do what we entrusted to no one else: cut the living crap out of it.

He trimmed the azaleas, yew, red cedar, Chinese juniper, and black and white pines. He brought his ladder and shears. If it wasn't pruning season, he busied himself by raking the bare dirt, stopping every now and then to look up at the sky. When I handed him a monthly check, he laughed, perhaps wondering why we paid so much for what he thought was so little. But we'd learned this much about a Zen garden: it's not what you put in, it's what you take out.

One day, he came carrying a bucket filled with chalky liquid, a concoction he had mixed at home. The big pine was sick with who knows what, but he had a tonic he wanted to try. He poured the medicine around the root line, then held up a crooked finger. "It takes one year to see if it lives." He thought again. "Maybe two."

The next week we received a typed letter in a hand-addressed envelope.

Dear loyal customer,

I have been in the hospital since Monday and will be undergoing surgery on Friday. After surgery, I will be out of commission for two to three weeks due to recovery. I would like to continue to work for you in your garden after my recovery and hope you can be patient until then. I do apologize for this inconvenience.

Sincerely,
Mr. Jeffery Isobe

Two weeks later, we received another.

Dear Mrs. Miller,

I would like to take this time to inform you of my resignation as your gardener due to an unfortunate discovery of a potentially terminal illness. My illness will require extended treatment and recovery, and I am unsure that my ability to perform my duties will ever return. In addition to considering my age, this is my only option.

It has been a pleasure to work for you and I do apologize for any inconvenience this may cause.

Sincerely,
Mr. Jeffery Isobe

Five months passed before we received one more letter, this time from his son. Mr. Isobe had died, at age eighty-three. Old buddhas do things the old way. They face the wind that sweeps away birth and death, before and after, beginning and end.

"In birth there is nothing but birth and in death there is nothing but death," Dogen said. "Accordingly, when birth comes, face and actualize birth. When death comes, face and actualize death. Do not avoid them or desire them."

Dogen's view of death was the same as Buddha's view of death: quite literal. We are born and we die. Anyone can see that, but Buddhism takes a closer look. Usually we think life begins with a momentous bang (so long ago we can't remember) and ends with a whimper (so long from now we aren't worried), but the Buddhist view is a bit different. Neither life nor death is a one-time shot. We are born and we die six billion times a day, and the entire universe along with us. Really! What we experience as just one measly little life is actually the world's biggest light show appearing and disappearing with such inconceivable speed that we can't perceive it. Each of us, each moment, is like a blazing solar flare or starburst: gone by the time we read about it.

Even though I can't express it, you know what I mean. Sometimes, right in the middle of an ordinary day, you feel sadness and longing. You have a deep sense of your own disappearance.

I'm writing this on the eighteenth anniversary of Maezumi Roshi's death. He was visiting his brother in Tokyo and stayed up late drinking, succumbing one more time to the shadow of habit. Sometime in the night, he sunk beneath the bathwater and disappeared. Beyond that, no one knows. I ask him questions he does not answer.

I had seen him months before, a week before his birthday, his sixty-fourth. Knowing the occasion, I wanted to leave a little something behind, a poem or a line inscribed when inspiration arrived. Nothing arrived, so I copied a story from a book I carried with me, a collection of stories by William Maxwell entitled *All the Days and Nights*. The book was a newfound treasure, and I had read it continually after hearing the delicate, eightysomething voice of the author on the car radio one night, saying, "I'm astonished that there always is a story, but first it has to come out of the absolutely emptied mind."

The story I copied for him was called "The Man Who Lost His Father." I put it inside a blank card with a picture of a blooming rose.

Maezumi had begun to fade. During our talks, he seemed to be taking stock, letting go of the relationships he could not repair or revive. "I will have one living line," he said about the legacy of his teaching, before thinking again. "Maybe two." Some seeds grow and some don't, according to conditions. They take root and spread, or not. If I'd thought about it back then, his estimate would have seemed pessimistic, but now that I've spent time under the oak, I see how life goes.

As is the Buddhist custom, a memorial service was held forty-nine days after his death. The late-summer day was cloudless and hot. People congregated on the baked pavement outside the auditorium to offer incense before a three-foot-tall picture of Maezumi. Up close, I could see that the harsh, slanting sunlight was melting the emulsion of the photograph, which stuck in wet spots to the encasing glass. The image was coming undone.

Inside, a procession of officiants entered to the sounds of a drum, the ringing of a bell, and the bellow of a conch shell. Japan had sent a bevy of Zen roshis in their ceremonial raiment and headdresses. The altar shone with arrangements of gold-plated lotus stems. As a spectacle, it seemed ill-fitting. Maezumi was not a showman.

At the end, attendants brought a box on stage and ignited its contents. Inside were messages collected from students. On my square of paper, I'd written words that had entered my skin when I'd heard Roshi speak them one winter morning as a memorial to his own father, reciting his own translation of a verse of Dogen's. From where I was standing, I could see the shine on his cheeks. He was crying.

> Midnight on the lake.
> No wind. No waves.
> The empty boat is flooded with moonlight.

Afterward, I'd gone into private interview, or *dokusan*, with Roshi and repeated the verse back, as though that alone was enough to convey my appreciation. He had smiled and spoken softly. "Where does the moonlight go?"

The smoke from burning paper drifted up, and it was gone.

For now, the pines are standing.

Part Three

LETTING GO

Make the effort of no effort.

CHAPTER 13

FRUIT
Swallowing Whole

I forgot the way I had come.
— HANSHAN

The buds appear in early winter and bloom throughout early spring. Theirs is the perfume of youth, the scent of morning. They number in the thousands, perfect star-shaped flowers caressed by eager breezes until nearly all of them loosen and fall. Those left behind — about one in a hundred — have been spared by the iffy wind and weather. They stay on the branch until they form a tiny fruit, hard and green, hidden among the dark leaves. Plumped on full sun and fed by deep water, they grow round and soft. Their skin becomes thin; their color turns radiant.

One tree can produce up to three hundred oranges a year. Mature fruit lasts for months on a branch without ruin, long enough for two crops to be stored on the tree at once: the old and the new. Pick an orange from a tree in my front yard, and its rind may be dirty or blemished, the color uneven, slightly shriveled, bulbous, shrunken. No two are alike. But under the layers of skin, scars, and dust, there is goodness, you see, pure goodness untempered by time. Once you taste it, you know for sure.

If you were offered a glass filled with life at its undiluted prime, would you refuse, preferring to gnaw on the bitter rind? That's what we do when we cannot move past the past: we keep swallowing the sour and never reach the sweet.

To know myself fully, I do not have to ponder the infinity of stars. I do not have to plumb the eternity of time. I only have to reach up and pluck the fruit from the bony end of a branch.

Of all the splendors in this patch of paradise, these old trees are most dear to me. They are susceptible to disease, afflicted by parasites and flies, brittle and arthritic. On appearance, they've exhausted their stay. But season after season they carry on. Their aroma is always fresh; their taste wakes me up. Oranges are in my blood. They are the family business. My grandfather grew oranges, and he taught me how to eat them. He was the best grandfather you could ever have. The best ancestors teach you to forget, and when you learn their secrets, they give you the best reason to forgive.

Many years ago, a family of three — my grandparents and their young son, my father — made their way from Illinois to California. I don't know the particulars, because the particulars remained unspoken. I don't know if they came by train or automobile. I don't know how many days it took, the time of year, or even the year. I don't know their ages or circumstances, their moods or motivations, whether they waved good-bye at a station or were met by someone who stepped through a screen door onto a front porch when the old Ford pulled into view.

I know little more than this: Illinois was the irredeemable past, and California was the eternal future.

Otherwise I've invented their story the way we invent all stories: from old photographs and fantasy, the dim recollection of things I might have seen or heard but more than likely only imagined.

I'm guessing that my grandparents stopped first in a place called Moorpark, where my father entered school. I can date this from the report cards saved by his mother in a keepsake box that was handed down to me. Her son was a good reader, a good speller, good with sums, and more than satisfactory in all ways except in one area of comportment, "school savings." By this one mark I recognize my full-grown father, who never held a penny he couldn't spend.

The family tried running a turkey farm, which failed. Four stashed report cards trace the hops they made across the valley in search of steady work. And then, in 1941, my father entered fifth grade in a red schoolhouse set deep in the orange groves between the migrant towns of Piru and Fillmore. They had arrived at a place to stay.

The Second World War had begun in Europe. America would soon enter. Oddly, things were looking up for the down-and-out.

They bought a plot carved from the endless groves

outside town, off a two-lane rut of a country road. They built a house: four rooms, three porches. It was plain. One side faced the valley; one side faced the mountain. Over that patch of earth the sun rose and set a billion times, the seasons took a million turns, and the wind dried ten million billion tears. They called it the "old place."

For my first twelve years, it was heaven. In those days I naturally had a child's sense of time. So I never questioned why my grandparents lived without a past, why there were no stories or traditions. The only photographs were of us. They didn't reminisce, and they fell out with distant cousins. Grandpa gave a swordsman's retort to the questions I couldn't help but ask. *Where did you come from? What was it like?*

"If there was anything worth remembering, we never would have left."

From him, I learned the miracle of love and the blessing of atonement. We can travel through time to reconcile the past and liberate the future. We only need to forget the way we came.

All evil karma ever committed by me since of old,
On account of my beginningless greed, anger, and
    ignorance,
Born of my body, mouth, and thought,
Now I atone for it all.

It can be unnerving to come across this verse, which is routinely chanted in Zen ceremonies when we take precepts, or vows, and as part of the monthly ritual of atonement. Gone are the sweetness and light, the fairy dust and moonbeams that might first attract us to Buddhism. Things suddenly take a serious turn. *Evil?* But I'm a nice person. *Karma?* It wasn't my fault! *Ignorant?* Who are you calling ignorant?

The verse is not a confession of sin or an admission of wrongdoing. It is a statement of responsibility. *I can make my life whole, and only I can do it.* In performing atonement, we acknowledge the suffering caused by our own ignorant view of ourselves as separate from the world we inhabit. Our ignorance of the truth gives rise to greed and anger. The verse serves the same purpose as all Zen chants, which is to transport us beyond the self-centered view that judges, blames, sets boundaries, destroys peace, and splinters the world into opposing sides — our egocentric mind. It affirms the aspect of ourselves that is eternally present, selfless, generous, patient, and compassionate — our Buddha mind.

The voice that speaks these words has the power to stop suffering in its tracks. It has the ability to instantly restore harmony simply by invoking it *now*. It is an awesome responsibility, but it takes only an instant.

Yes, yes, I know. What happened before wasn't your fault. It was too soon. It was too late. It was too much. They didn't ask. They didn't tell. You didn't know. It was unfair. It hurt. They lied. You cried. It was a mistake. It was a crime. But that was then.

We forgive because we *can*. And we forget because we *must*, or we condemn ourselves to lifetimes of pain.

So forget the story you tell yourself about your parents,

the story you tell yourself about your childhood, the story of absence and lack. Forget the birth story, the death story, the divorce story, the story you keep repeating, the story you'll never forget. Forget that story, and do not replace it with another.

Forget what might have been and what might yet be. The past is gone and the future will arrive on schedule.

Forget what you thought. Forget what you felt. Today is the tonic for yesterday. Now is the only cure for then. Forget, and you will know genuine gratitude. Gratitude is the fruit of letting go.

And don't worry. You'll always encounter what you need to know when you need to know it, so go ahead and forget this too.

∽

Luckily, teachers keep repeating themselves. My current teacher regularly recites a set of instructions given to him by Maezumi Roshi in the early days of his own training. At the time, he didn't think much of it. Wisdom teachings seep slowly up from the ground by the roots, spread through the branches, and plop into your hands right when you're ready to swallow them. Here are Maezumi's Three Admonitions:

1. *Don't deceive yourself.* We're all taught to refrain from lying, and we usually interpret this to mean not lying to *others*. In truth, every time we tell a lie, we lie to ourselves, and we are the only ones consistently fooled. We can seldom con others for as long as we con ourselves. My greatest deceit is the deceit of a separate self, with all my ego-reinforcing

views. Without practice, my views amount to little more than self-congratulation or self-criticism, and both are lies. Truth is totally dependent on my own clarity.

2. *Don't make excuses for yourself.* The list of all the people and things I blame is endless. Blaming external, or even internal, conditions for what I do or don't do is dualistic. As long as I'm casting blame elsewhere, I am reinforcing my own wrongheaded view as separate. I must begin to see that any excuse I make for myself is a self-deception. The power to change is mine only. Waking up is up to me. The responsibility for my life begins right here, and only when I stop excusing myself does my life benefit everyone and everything.

3. *Take responsibility for yourself.* I've got to admit, sometimes I feel like the most responsible person on the planet. But that's not nearly responsible enough. To take complete responsibility for yourself is to no longer tell yourself lies or make excuses as if you were a powerless victim of your own life. Taking responsibility for yourself means taking responsibility for everything. It's a big job, but it's already in your hands, so take good care of it.

In these three little instructions you will find both the seed and the fruit of continuous awakening: nothing other than you.

෧◦

Once you taste the living truth, you are never again fooled by the imitation flavored drink in a carton. The picture on the front is very appealing, so they sell a lot, but it's not the real thing.

Grandpa showed me how to peel an orange. Hold the fruit in one hand and the pocketknife in the other. First, score a circle in the rind around the navel below and the stem on top. Draw the blade down the sides in vertical strokes all around the whole, no deeper than the skin, an inch between each cut. Be careful. Go slowly. Do not harm the flesh.

Lift off the top and bottom pieces. Pull each section of rind away from the fruit. It will come easily, and with it, the pith. Wedge your thumb into the center and splay the fruit wide open. There will be ten or so segments — enough to share. Using the knife, lift each piece apart, balanced on the edge of the blade. Offer the first taste to someone close by, then take one for yourself.

She was a teenager. He was married. It took two years for him to undo his vows, be banished from the church, and give the boy his name. There is no way to know the cause or assign the blame. Somehow they ruined each other, and having only each other, they left everything else behind. They went far away and built a house for the lie. They made a place for the shame. Up from the dust grew what I came to know as paradise.

The truth came out after both grandparents were dead, when lost relatives were reunited and a comment from an uncle gave my middle-aged father the kind of shock that hollows you out and makes perfect sense of the missing pieces.

My mother told me while it was still a secret, hoping that my father would one day tell his daughters himself. One of my sisters saw him crumpled in his chair — the daddy chair we weren't allowed to sit in — head in his hands, calling himself a name that we called him all the time, just never out loud. It's an epithet that comes easily to mind for anyone who is liberal with anger, stingy with kindness, and hard to like, but in our case it was true. Our dad was a bastard.

I was already grown up and gone. He wrote a letter, and in between the lines of his handwriting, delivering the hard truth he was making his own, was something else. He was asking for my forgiveness. This was as close as he would ever come to making atonement. Could I forgive the stain of his birth, the lie of his life, his demons, his failings? I imagined he was asking what his own father did in a half-century of hiding: *Could anyone ever love someone as terrible as me?*

Our task is to answer this plea even when it doesn't come; our task is to forgive continuously and drop the burden of holding on to *anything*.

So again I lift my voice from the deep well of pure awareness: I forgive all the fathers, all the children, all the mothers, everyone. I atone for all I've done and didn't do; thought and didn't think; said and didn't say. I alone can wipe the record clean; make the broken whole. I was taught to eat an orange right off the tree, let the past be past, the dead be dead, and live among the living right now. Because every day is a new day on the old place.

CHAPTER 14

FLOWERS
Love Is Letting Go

What shall be my legacy?
The blossoms of spring.
— RYŌKAN

They don't make it past spring, the camellia flowers, but oh, what a beautiful spring. Their blooms appear in one energetic burst, when the winter's color has dulled to gray. They arrive when it's dark and cold and you've ceased to believe in the promise of April or May. They pop up when time has frozen and you have turned blue, yes, blue, with the sad certainty that *nothing ever changes around here*. You see a wink of color and turn to see a lady dressed in red. She tosses off her beauty in the hour of its perfection, and the flowers carpet the ground where you walk.

Flowers are love's perfect offering. They do not ask to be appreciated. They expect nothing in return. They just let go.

Camellia japonica is a mainstay of Japanese temple gardens but was once avoided around private homes. That's because the flower has no life span to speak of. It does not adorn the branch for long but falls off at its peak. You can see why some people would think this peculiar feature unappealing, even disturbing, but the Buddhists saw a lesson in this. (We see a lesson in everything.) In life there is death. In form, there is emptiness. In eternity there is fragility. What are you holding onto? What will you leave behind? Like the blossoms in their evanescent beauty, throw yourself into this moment and leave no trace.

"It's not a flower garden," I say about this place, meaning this isn't the kind of garden where you fill a bed with blooming annuals and replace them when they fade. But then again, that's not quite right. This *is* a flower garden and it's a bed of roses too. I don't have to do anything, and yet flowers are appearing all the time: azalea, jasmine, and wisteria in spring; agapanthus, water lilies, and day lilies in summer; camellia, bird of paradise, and orange blossoms in winter; floribunda roses and gardenias nearly all year long. Even the dandelions count. By some mysterious and unerring hand flowers all appear right on time. They seed the fruit. They feed the bees and butterflies; they sweeten the breeze. They are subtle and selfless, here and gone, appearing and disappearing, part and parcel of life's perennial display. By this definition *everything* is a flower; by this lesson, *all* is love. Life is indeed love, continually pouring itself into itself — for my benefit and delight, I might add — but by my egocentric thinking I can be blind to the gift.

Love is abundant, but if you're like me you may live a

good part of the time thinking otherwise. That's because love doesn't always fit your idea of love. It doesn't feel like you think it should. It doesn't go your way. When I move through my own full house and go virtually unnoticed by my distracted cohabitants; when I set a meal on the table and no one answers my call, takes a seat, or applauds; when I hang up someone else's clothes, rinse someone else's dishes, straighten someone else's mess, and fix someone else's mistakes, leaving no one the wiser; when I cry for someone else's pain and sweat someone else's small stuff; when the neighbor doesn't invite me over and the party goes on without me; when the critics are brutal and the fans are slow to muster, I'm rather convinced that I've gotten a raw deal from love, that I'm party to an uneven exchange. But that's wrongheaded. This is my universe, and all the love in it is mine. If I detect a shortage, it's because I've been picky, close-minded, or stingy. Can I love a bit better and give a bit more? Considering that I'm the only one stopping me, well, yes, I can.

Whatever you love will bring you to the final test of love: letting go of what you think love is.

೧౧

Buddhists don't try to cause trouble, but one thing that troubles people about Buddhism is the concept of nonattachment. That's because we think attachment means love, and we think love means *I can't live without you*. We are always hung up on our self-serving notions — what I need, what I want, what I like, what I think, what is best, what is right — and that's the cause of suffering. We attach to those ideas as though they were life itself. The truth is never the phony thing we attach to in our heads. The truth is *as it is*.

Buddha taught what he called the Four Noble Truths. He taught truth as it is, complete and universal. He called it noble because there's nothing truer than *what is*. You don't have to believe this is true because you experience it every time things don't go your way.

1. Life is suffering. *Things change.*
2. The origin of suffering is attachment. *It hurts when things change.*
3. The cessation of suffering is attainable. *Accept that things change.*
4. There is a way out of suffering. *By changing yourself.*

When we try to imagine what it means to overcome our attachments, we picture cruel and unfeeling indifference. But that is never the outcome of overcoming attachments. That is never the outcome of accepting what happens. That is never the outcome of allowing people and things to be as they are. The outcome of nonattachment is love.

I don't have to preach this. You know it yourself by waking up to life as it is. Your children grow up and grow distant. They might upset, alarm, and even despise you, but your eyes still flicker at the sight of them. Your parents grow old, enfeebled, and afraid, dependent and encumbering, but you care for them. Sickness comes, disaster strikes, and seasons change. Everything falls apart no matter how hard you've tried: all that forethought, planning, and prevention! This life of ours is strewn with faded blooms. You didn't sign up for the hard part, but this is the way it is. How will you love what you don't even like? There's only one way: selflessly.

When you act with compassion, all your doing is undo-ing — undoing ignorance, suffering, fear, anger, exploita-tion, alienation, injury, blame, you name it — simply by undoing the stingy hold you keep on yourself. Thinking *poor me* impoverishes your entire world.

When my daughter was about six years old, someone asked her what it was like to have a mom who was a Zen priest.

"She screams a lot," she said. It wasn't the answer they were expecting. There were polite chuckles all around.

I can comfort myself with the fact that children only remember when their parents scream, not when their par-ents don't. Silence, after all, is a nonevent. No matter what I was hollering about, I wish I'd had the presence of mind to let it go. I wish I'd dropped my rage, fear, frustration, or despair: whatever illusory part of me I was cherishing at the time. I wish love could be my legacy instead, the way a camellia launches its blossoms into the oblivion of time without causing a quiver of pain. No one ever notices when a flower has fulfilled its purpose in life, just as no one ever regrets a moment lost to love.

"He was the kindest person I ever met." These words were spoken by Maezumi Roshi's widow after his death, after their public troubles and private pain, and after she was left alone to raise three children. When flowers fall, you realize the gift of their presence by their absence.

Maezumi introduced me to a dimension of love that we do not often experience. His love was not administered in the guise of charity or sympathy. He did not serve as a counselor, advocate, or intermediary. He had no suggestions for how I could improve myself. He simply sat in a room. When he rang a bell, you could enter, sit in front of him, and be seen. The two of us would talk a little and laugh or cry: whatever. Gradually, I would relax and stop trying to make an impression. His kindness was the profound kindness of seeing a person or thing completely, without judgment. I learned two things by this: that it is rare to be seen and that seeing without judging is an act of love.

Zen practice is facing yourself as you are. And by accepting yourself, you come to accept everything. Self-consciousness dissolves and separation disappears. Free of deception, you are no longer afraid to be yourself. You are no longer afraid of much of anything. There is nothing to hide; no self-image to defend; nothing to assemble, control, or avoid. It's simply a matter of taking care of what appears in front of you.

Whatever appears in front of you is your liberation — that is, until you judge it. Then you imprison yourself again.

"Be intimate with your life," Maezumi used to say, over and over, and in every way he could. Meditation is about cultivating intimacy with your life — not intellectually, as in *I get it*, but literally, as in *I am it* — intimacy with your breath, your sweat, your body odor, the pain in your back and knees, the crazy rage and riot in your head, and the saliva at the back of your throat. Intimacy with food and sleep, light and air, earth and sky, everyone and everything.

When you leave nothing out, there's no end to it. This intimacy goes far beyond the companionship and gratification we seek from another person. Keeping company with yourself changes the expectations you place on a relationship. You see firsthand what it means to take responsibility for your own fulfillment, and you experience love of a different kind — compassion, which arises spontaneously as your true nature.

When you practice Zen formally with a group, you have the opportunity to sit in silence for a day or more alongside someone you hardly know. This is a tiny bit uncomfortable. Maybe the person next to you uses scented soap or aftershave, and it makes your eyes itch or nose run. Maybe she breathes loudly. Or he is restless, and every time he wiggles it ticks you off. You can hear her stomach gurgle and her belly groan. He sneezes or coughs and you think he'll make you sick. How rude! He isn't considering you at all! You hate him already.

Eventually, your mind will grow quiet and your concentration will deepen. You will share space without the judgments and expectations we usually impose on those around us and be in relationships that are not based on what another person is doing for you or how she is pleasing you. At the end of the time together, you might be inclined to do what I do: turn to the stranger sitting nearby, smile, and spontaneously say, "I love you." The thing is, I really mean it. Is it possible to love in this way? Yes, from the very bottom of your heart and mind, when you let go of the all the reasons *why not to*, it is more than possible. It is effortless.

In the zendo, after the dawn sitting block, when you've

dozed through the first ninety minutes of *zazen*, there is a chant we repeat called the Verse of the Kesa, which means "verse of the robe." At this point some people put on their *rakusu*, which is a bib worn by lay practitioners, or their *okesa*, which is the sari that priests wear over their robes. Even if you don't wear either of those things you'll say the verse just the same. Whether it is long or short, could be worn by a priest or a plumber, what you wear in *zazen* marks you as a student of the Way. More than that, your *zazen is* the *zazen* of the Buddha. Talk about intimate.

As a Zen practitioner you'll do and say weird things you may not understand, aping them awkwardly or halfheartedly, just trying to get the words and gestures down. Having someone explain them to you is a bit of a disservice, because it can trivialize the dharma into something that you *get* instead of something that you *are*. But even so, one day you'll realize that it's not mumbo jumbo.

The *rakusu* or the *okesa* — whatever you wear to practice in — is your banner of freedom. It's like a superhero cape that liberates you from yourself. The Verse of the Kesa is a song of love, your vow to transform greed, anger, and ignorance into selfless compassion. It might seem ironic that we hang something around our necks to express freedom, or that we don archaic garments in the name of formlessness, but Zen is funny like that. It covers all the bases.

> Vast is the robe of liberation.
> A formless field of benefaction.
> I wear the Tathagata's teaching.
> Saving all sentient beings.

You'll say this so many times that you no longer have to think about it. When you stop having as much trouble with other people, you'll have a hunch that it's working. When you stop noticing any difference at all, it's *really* working.

Buddhism asks big questions about birth and death, cause and effect, emptiness and form, delusion and enlightenment. I just hope you're not actually thinking about any of that stuff, because Buddhism is fundamentally about something that requires no thought.

Every time I meet with my current teacher in *dokusan*, or face-to-face interview, we talk about my practice. After a little back and forth, he'll wrap up the interview with what sounds like small talk.

"How's your family?"

I roll my eyes and repeat the usual about how worried or anxious I am, how busy, how burdened, how bothered, and then I realize. *That* was the big question.

The big question is always a little question. What's it like to have a Zen priest for a mother?

One time after a mountain retreat, Maezumi asked me to come to his home nearby and meet his family. At the time there was only one phone on the property of the Zen Center (this was before cell phones would add another layer of egocentric disengagement to modern life), a pay phone strung up outside the bathhouse, and when it rang, someone ran up to the dorm to fetch me. I was packing to leave.

"Roshi is calling for you!" the messenger said, out of breath.

I was feeling pretty special on the way downhill to take the call, but when I heard his invitation, I had to say no. It was impossible, what with the drive to LAX and a plane to catch. Perhaps he didn't understand how impractical it was for me. Maybe he didn't grasp how far I had to travel or what I had to do. I thought he was a little naive to the ways of the world I lived in. No, I couldn't come but maybe some other time. We all know how that kind of thinking turns out.

In between the self-important student who has no time and the mom who terrifies her kid, I've gotten a good look at what I hold dearest — *myself*. It's what I must let go of completely before it's time to go. Then this one life will have flowered into something beautiful without my getting in the way.

One more thing.

"Mom, you don't have to keep telling me because I know."

I love you.

CHAPTER 15

LEAVES
The Age of Undoing

When you leave the way to the way, you attain the Way.
— DOGEN ZENJI

In the end, what ties everything together is how predictably it falls apart.

Like everyone, I have seen heaps of leaves all my life, but I never really noticed the part when they fall to the earth. When you watch a tree drop its leaves, it changes you. It alters your ambition and interrupts your agenda. There's nothing like the sight of falling leaves to give you a glimpse of reality, especially if it's in your own backyard.

It was my forty-first birthday. I was looking out the garden window in our guest room, also called our office (it would be lost to either use when a baby took up residence a year later). I was alone, in the middle of the day, amid September's melancholy stillness, with nothing to do except give undue consideration to the sad landscape of my recent loss. Three months earlier I'd left my job, sunk my savings into this decrepit house, sacrificed my slim claim to fame and greatness, and brought myself down to earth. And for what? I was no clearer on the *why*. Then it began to rain, a translucent veil that fell like lace from the crown of the sky. Did this even qualify as rain? I had to wonder, being a transplant from the land of whip-cracking cloudbursts and tornado warnings with sudden raging floods that crested two feet higher than your front door. *That* was rain.

I remember this event not because of the birthday, one of many that would come after the year I wanted to stop counting, but because of the delicate mist that carried the first leaves down from the sycamores, leaves still green and as wide across as my two hands. What a show — the water, the light, and the leaves gliding into the soft landing of letting go.

I had lived for forty-one years before I ever saw a tree lose its leaves. After that, everything I saw was a falling leaf. Everything came down.

This is partly because of the sycamores that tower over the western edge of the garden. There are three of them. There used to be more. The earliest photos of this place depict a shady glade dotted with young sycamores. At some point, a more moderate sense of proportion prevailed, and all but the three survivors were removed.

Sycamores shed everything. A hundred feet tall with a seventy-foot spread, our sycamores drop leaves all through fall and early winter and again in spring — the result of a nonlethal fungus that afflicts the first leaves of the year. The trees drop seed pods and bark. None of these losses limit the trees' terrific growth or life span. Sycamores generate perpetual work and worry for the groundskeepers beneath, and so I'm afraid they are not much admired. Ours are disfigured by disdain. Halfway up their height, the trunks take a ninety-degree turn and extend ten feet *horizontally* before resuming their upward thrust. A tree trimmer told me this misshape was the result of topping off. Fifty years ago someone got fed up and lopped off the leafy heads of these old girls. Wouldn't this have killed them? The tree guy laughed. Apparently it's impossible to kill a California sycamore, no matter how hard you try. Eventually you let go and just live with them. What a useful thing to do.

In the seasons after that first gentle douse, I would lose quite a bit. I would lose whole months to raking and scooping piles of leaves from the ponds. I would lose my parents. The loss of one parent seemed greater than the other, but both deaths would come as blessings. I would kiss goodbye to a baby who kept growing up, and to another never born. I would lop off my hair and overlook my abs. I would forego my not-quite Michelle Obama upper arms and find instead that they had turned entirely into an old lady's sagging underarms. Along the way, my gray would grow out and I would not deny it. My tube of under-eye concealer would dry up and I would not replace it. My earlobes would lengthen and my neck would crease. I would move in and out of menopause, an event that leaves me without any lasting sentiment to share. It's not so bad to find yourself free of the effort to overcome your life. It's not so bad.

I came to the garden just in time to enter the age of

undoing. Surprisingly, it's the age where the most amazing transformations take place. Every single leaf drops every single year from a sycamore, and it is the end of nothing. I came to the garden and found the shortest course to strength and freedom. I learned that all my faith lies in the path of least resistance — in the humble power and aching grace of letting go.

⁓

A modern master, Yasutani Roshi, used to tell his Western students not to do Zen the way they did everything else, not to make it so difficult. Not to aim so high (or low), want so much (or little), hurt so bad (or good), judge so quickly and then stop dead: *I tried it but it doesn't work for me.* Zen works precisely by not working for you in the old ego-aggrandizing ways. Of course, it's difficult enough to sit still and be quiet but not half as difficult as we make it out to be. Nothing is as difficult as we make it out to be, but by our thinking we make it grievously so.

It seems I've lived as though there were two of me. Right where I stand is me as I am. Opposite me is another me, one I've never met. She is quite wonderful, charming, and accomplished. She sits longer, for instance, *every day*, and eats much less. She says and does nothing she regrets. She went to the exercise class I skipped; she didn't even glance at the dessert menu. She has all the potential I have misspent: youth, for instance, time, patience, and kindness. All the while that we have traveled side by side, she has taken a different road, one I've never seen. I am taunted by her perfection. The problem for me, you see, is not that I compare myself to you, but that I compare myself to some-one who doesn't even exist: *the other me*. I will never know contentment until I confront her, disarm her, and lop off her leafy head. She creates way too much work for the grounds-keeper beneath.

I always imagined this other me to be happier than the real me, which made me feel lacking and sad. I won-der: Do we grieve most for what we've lost or for what we never had?

Letting go of her, I find I've lost nothing. The entire world was all mine to begin with. She was just hitching a ride. I can't believe I put up with her nonsense for so long.

Not all of it, but a good part of life's distress is conjured out of anxious expectation, cruel judgment, painful rumina-tion, or maudlin self-indulgence. Try letting go of all that. If you don't do Zen the way you do everything else, how will it be? *It will be real*. What a relief to accept that you will never get your act together. Then it is no longer an act. You can begin to live as you really are.

In the name of authenticity, I researched how many leaves are produced by a mature sycamore tree. (I wanted to give some heft to the hardship, not yet convinced that you feel my pain.) A healthy sycamore can hold two hun-dred thousand leaves each year. Cleaning up after three mature trees over the sixteen years I've been here means I have hauled more than *twenty-eight hundred pounds of fallen leaves*.

I could handle it. It wasn't too much. It didn't over-whelm me because I didn't lift all three tons at once. I picked them up the same way they fell: one by one. We can handle anything because we only have to handle it a moment at a time. That's how we live, and that's how we die.

My mother came to visit after she'd had two rounds of chemo for ovarian cancer. Her hair had grown back, only it didn't look like her hair. It was dense, dark, and curly like a crocheted cap. I couldn't get used to it. What helps us to let go is that appearances change so completely. Nature is kind in that way — we can't say we haven't been warned. Most leaves wither and fade before they fall, fulfilling every bit of their purpose.

She didn't look like my mom, but she was still my mom, cheerful and uncomplaining, even though her odds weren't any better after treatment. The only thing she wished for was to be free of the numbness in her feet. The doctors said this was a side effect of the chemo. She soaked her feet and I rubbed them. Nothing helped.

"I just want to feel like I did before." She let herself whine just a little, as if a pair of normal feet wasn't too much to ask for. *Before* is always too much to ask for. In the next few months she'd have more surgery and chemo, lose most of her colon, her appetite, and too much weight; the ability to chew and digest; the strength to resist the pain or refuse the painkillers, until at last she was released from the instinct to draw another breath.

When you've done all you can do, undo.

Life and death move by their own propulsion: straight on, straight on. We may not know how the road will turn but the direction is always clear. In her death, my mother showed me the dignity that arises from indignity, the grace we find in falling from grace. From the ground, it looks as if leaves die, but to the leaf, freed from a useless stem, it feels like flying.

～

Freedom can be a frightening prospect. It is frightening up until the moment you are actually free. That's when you realize it is the *thought* of freedom that terrifies you, because that's all that fear is: a thought.

There is a beginning meditation practice — which is profoundly advanced — called "counting the breath." Once you have positioned yourself to sit on a cushion, a bench, or a chair, you settle the mind in the *hara*, or the gut, and you start to count your inhalations and exhalations. The way I do this is to count an inhalation "one" and an exhalation "two" then an inhalation "three" and an exhalation "four." The instructions are to continue in this way until you reach ten. Sounds clear and simple enough. The truth is that when you try to do it, you find that you can't get much beyond four or five before the mind darts across a meadow and over a fence, builds up speed, and takes off into the beyond. When you find that you are lost in thought, you start back at one and keep going.

In this beginning meditation, which becomes even more difficult with the frequency of your practice, you spend a considerable amount of time trying to get to ten. *Come on, get to ten,* you tell yourself, *get to ten! Get somewhere, you slowpoke!*

The thing is, should you ever get to ten, the instructions are to start back at one. The ten and the one have no merit or meaning, you see. But try believing that for yourself.

My teacher keeps tweaking my practice. He's holding my feet to the fire.

"Maezen," he tells me, "get to zero." Nothing to grasp, in free flight, without leaving the ground.

◦◦◦

Under the umbrella of the mighty sycamores, the fragile Japanese maple is hardly noticeable until one week in November, when it turns itself on fire with flaming red leaves that shrivel into themselves and disappear.

The year after a girl turns thirteen is frightening. At least it is for her mother. Here you are, saying and doing the same clumsy things you've always said and done, only now there is someone sitting beside you in the car or on the sofa, nearly your size or taller, who turns her head and stares at you with a look you don't recognize. In that blankness you think you see what you never dreamed would shadow your baby's face: a complete stranger.

"I feel like we've lost a daughter," my husband said.

"They come back," say mothers far wiser than I. The evidence is plainly on their side. Not just for a hundred years, but for *four hundred million years*, leaves have left the trees for an entire gloomy winter, which was nonetheless no longer than a winter. Swept bare, their arms are not dead, just empty. A naked tree seems elegantly impervious, but perhaps it's just in shock to find itself alone again, naturally.

"Make the effort of no effort," Maezumi Roshi said. The effort of no effort is the hardest effort of all. This is the effort that you owe to everything and everyone in your world, which is, after all, a natural world, with natural intelligence, harmony, rhythm, and wisdom. Trust it. Be patient. We do not manufacture summer or winter, nor do we love by clinging to the way things used to be. You might as well try to tape a leaf back on a tree.

At some point, your children will no longer baby you. Your parents will no longer bother you. Good teachers hold your feet to the fire until you let go.

Empty-handed, the masters say, we attain the Way. This is *samadhi* in action, the healing power of your peaceful presence, resisting nothing, adding nothing, thinking nothing, enabling you to say good-bye to your mother and hello to your daughter, even though neither of them answers. Sit quietly and enter the fullness of time, where the seasons advance in one viewing. Know that leaves bud and break. Flowers bloom and burst. Fruit softens and drops. Earth is our mother. She heals even the last fall.

The gardener is not afraid.

CHAPTER 16

WEEDS
A Flourishing Practice

Empty handed, holding a hoe.
— MAHASATTVA FU

Paradise is a patch of weeds.

What loyal friends, these undesirables that infiltrate the lawn, insinuate between the cracks, and luxuriate in the deep shade of my neglect. Weeds are everywhere, showing up every day. I have quite a bit of help around here, but weeds are my most reliable underlings. Where would I be without them? I would run out of reasons to wake up every morning. I would lack motivation and direction. I might consider the job here done.

The job here is just beginning.

As if it isn't obvious enough, I must confess that in these sixteen years of gardening I have not yet learned how to garden. By this I mean that I do not know the chemistry of soils or the biology of compost. I have not learned the nomenclature; I do not know the right time or way to prune. My most useful tools are the ones farthest from my hands: sun and water. I have not planted a single thing still standing. In all this time in the yard I have cultivated no worthwhile skills, save one that is decidedly unskilled.

I weed.

I offer this up as a modest qualification because I have noticed how reluctantly most people bring themselves to the task. Weeding is not a popular pastime, even among gardeners. Weeds are the very emblem of aversion. Weeding doesn't produce a rewarding outcome. No grand finale, no big reveal. There's absolutely nothing to show for it. One spring I directed our revered Mr. Isobe to a troublesome spot in the backyard where tiny undesirables were spreading through the mondo grass. He squinted to see what I was pointing to. He did not share my distress but broke into laughter. "You want me to weed?" Perhaps he couldn't believe that someone of his stature would be asked to stoop to the occasion. Or perhaps I was just imagining what he meant. In any event, I was offended, and I didn't ask him again. The weeds were all mine.

While I was casting about for something to do *for the rest of my life*, as we like to characterize temporary forms of employment, I hit on a scheme. I'd seen how common it was for an otherwise respectable yard to be surrendered over to wilderness for the lack of a spade. And the worse it got, the worse it gets. I suggested to my husband that I start an enterprise — not for landscape design or decoration, for which I was unsuited — but just for weeding. I would call it "Just

Weeds." I would go over to people's houses every week and just pull weeds — probably weeds they didn't even know they had! I thought it was inspired, but he thought it was lame. So instead I do it every day for no pay. This is how your life becomes rich with purpose. You take care of things that lie right under your feet, and no one even notices.

The most common weeds in the yard are crabgrass, dandelion, and chickweed. The most common weeds in the world are greed, anger, and ignorance.

This is the way to weed. Anchor yourself low to the ground so you can get a good look at what you're dealing with. Use a spade to loosen the hardpack and go deeper. The next part is tricky. Take hold of the stem and apply your attention, allowing the root to release. Haste and carelessness will only aggravate the situation. Sometimes you can get the root on the first tug. Other times you'll just tear off the top. Even if you don't get it all the first time, that's okay. It may take two or three, ten or twenty, one hundred thousand or a million times, to get the root completely. Just keep going along like that, encountering the next weed that appears in front of you *for the rest of your life.*

Ten things to do to spare the garden from stubborn entanglements:

1. *Blame no one.* I could blame the yardman for the weeds. Or everyone who ever let them fester. In other words, I could blame the folks who aren't around for what they haven't done. I could blame the sun, the dirt, the wind, the seed, the rain, and

the shade. But what does any of that matter when
the spade is in my hands? Blame's central deceit is
that anyone or anything else is responsible for what
I think, feel, say, and do. Blame is a powerful barrier: like prickly thistle, it spreads pain and disaffec-
tion. So why toss fault around? To elevate my ego
and justify my self-righteousness, that's why. Watch
that you do not become attached to your version of
events. Blame turns the garden into a menace.

2. *Take no offense.* But I'm so good at taking offense,
usually at what someone doesn't even know he did.
That's because offense is an inside job. It requires
that we ascribe malice and meaning to empty words
or actions. Consider the energy we expend to pro-
long fictional injuries. How hard is it to get over
what's already over? I know: it's hard. But there's
a way.

3. *Forgive.* Forgiveness is the cure. Without it, we
sell the farm under our feet, subdividing common
ground into stingy little parcels that are good for
nothing. Forgiveness reconciles the rift between self
and other. Like property lines, the barrier between
us doesn't really exist except as a function of greed,
anger, or judgment. Forgive someone today —
forgive yourself today — and feel the fence lines
recede. Suddenly, it's much easier to move on.

4. *Do not compare.* There is no greener grass. There is
no other side. Your life is not a competition, a race,
or a chase. No one is ahead of you, and there is no
way to fall behind. Satisfy yourself with what you

have in hand. It may not look like much, but this right here is everything. And it's alive.

5. *Take off your gloves.* A nurseryman once told me, "A real gardener doesn't wear gloves." A gardener wears dirt, unafraid to get muddy, scratched, or stung, because hands are how we see, hear, and feel. Native intelligence flows through your fingertips. Wisdom is received in direct connection with the world, telling you how deep to dig and how hard to pull, when to gather and when to release. Self-defenses make you timid and clumsy. You can do without the layers of protection.

6. *Forget yourself.* The world needs fewer people to own their greatness and a few more to own their humility. So let's stop pretending. We are never *really* who we think we are; nor are we anywhere close to the ideal we strive for. My neighbors down the street installed expensive artificial turf on a strip of yard closest to the street. It's an uncanny like-ness. Each blade is a uniform height and color, so it never needs to be watered or cut. It passes as grass from a distance, but up close you can tell it's not real. Worse yet, weeds still crop up through the weave, and they are even harder to get rid of. When you can face reality without camouflage, yours is the face of compassion. What a sight for sore eyes! No longer obsessed with your self-image, you be-come genuine. Barefaced and open, your smile is easy; your eyes wide and bright. Nothing is beneath or beyond you. You can do the smallest things.

You carry peace wherever you go and share it with everyone, mindful that we're all doing our best, and headed in the same direction.

7. *Grow old*. It isn't easy; it's effortless.

8. *Have no answers*. If, as the ancients say, we are born and we die six billion times a day; if, as according to modern science, fifty million cells in your body will replace themselves in the time it takes for you to read this sentence, do you really have an answer for anything? In Zen, we don't find the answers; we lose the questions. It's impossible to comprehend the marvel of what we are or to understand the mystery of life's impeccable genius. Thankfully, there is no need. You don't have to know how your heart beats in order to get your mitral valve to open. You don't have to ace Anatomy 101 to move your arms and feet. The state of not-knowing does not imply a lack of learning; it is the totality of truth. You're already real, genuine, and functioning perfectly as you are. Weed out the confusion that comes from trying to understand. Don't think, and you will be grateful.

9. *Seek nothing*. "All who seek suffer," Buddhism teaches. "If there is no seeking, only then is there bliss." That gives you a pretty clear picture of where the suffering begins and ends. Just for one moment take my word that you lack nothing. That you're perfectly okay even when you're not okay. If you've recognized something in these pages that you want to underline and remember, it's because

you already know it. Have faith in yourself as the Way.

10. *Go back to 1.* The Buddha is still refining his practice.

❧

The old teachers called them "sweetgrasses," the overgrowth that beckons from the side of the road. Dense and shimmery, they are eye candy to the weary pilgrim but poisonous. Wander close and they'll make you sick. *Let me chew on this for a while* — anger, blame, guilt — *let me hide out in those brambles* — fear and worry — *let me lie down and go to sleep* — rumination and make-believe — *so I don't have to keep going.* The path leads on. There's no end in sight. You can only see what's right in front of you. The scenery may not seem interesting or the time productive. You get bored and look around for, well, something.

Shouldn't I be making progress? Going faster? Accomplishing more? Getting somewhere? Surely there's more to this trip than one measly breath at a time, one lousy foot in front of the other? I don't see what's so special about it.

We can lose our lives in these sidetracks: dwelling on the past and anticipating the future; judging, resisting, and debating with ourselves; falling again into the familiar ruts. To be fair, poison ivy isn't all bad: its berries feed foraging birds and wildlife. But you don't want to tromp around in it. In tiny doses, hemlock is medicinal. But don't make a meal of it.

When folks begin to practice, they can be set back by how hard it is. They might have expected to be good at it —

for certain, they expected something — but what they are good at is something else altogether.

Why is it so hard just to breathe? *Because you've been practicing holding your breath.*

Why is it so hard to keep my eyes open? *Because you've been practicing falling asleep.*

Why is it so hard to be still? *Because you've been practicing running amok.*

Why is it so hard to be quiet? *Because you've been practicing talking to yourself.*

Why is it so hard to pay attention? *Because you've been practicing inattention.*

Why is it so hard to relax? *Because you've been practicing stress.*

Why is it so hard to trust? *Because you've been practicing fear.*

Why is it so hard to have faith? *Because you've been trying to know.*

Why is it so hard to feel good? *Because you've been practicing feeling bad.*

Whatever you practice, you'll get very good at. You've been practicing these things forever. Take your own life as proof that practice works as long as you keep doing it. Just replace a harmful practice with one that does no harm.

The desperate traveler keeps going, and a change takes place. The landscape transforms from a jungle pocked with toxins into an open field. The interruptions are fewer, the diversions farther between. The sweetgrasses are left behind. We cultivate the field step-by-step: swinging breath like a hoe to clear the surface of mind, using *samadhi* like a spade to go deeper. What does it take to turn a pit of poison into paradise? We can say we know, but we still have to do it over and over again, and never quit.

After practicing *shikantaza*, just sitting, for forty years, Maezumi Roshi said, "I think I'm beginning to do it."

Every time I step into the garden, I've landed my dream job. Only it's not called "Just Weeds." It's just weeds, the business of a buddha. I think I'm beginning to do it.

CHAPTER 17

SONG
Not What You Know

What is this?
— *Blue Cliff Record*, case 51

What you think is an affliction is actually wisdom calling you home.

One morning, not too many years ago, the neighbor who lives behind us knocked on the front door. I knew who he was, but we'd never met face-to-face. He'd come the long way around so he could ask about something that was keeping him up at night.

"Are you raising livestock back there?"

The gentleman had lived beside the garden nearly all his life. His home was converted from the carriage house on the original estate. And now a beastly sound was haunting his sleep. It came from our side of the fence. Whatever the source, it stretched the bounds of guesswork. I could have said yes, I was raising an ox, but I knew what he was talking about, so the least I could do was make a good neighbor aware.

It was a frog that sounded like a bull, or maybe a bull that had the appearance of a frog, should we ever catch a glimpse. From his question, I could assume it was the first frog to have matured in this pond in many years. That out of twenty thousand eggs smeared like a distant galaxy across the surface of the water under a spring moon, a solitary survivor should rise up and evade every predator's grasp, outgrow the mouths of fish, outsmart the birds, outlast the raccoons, and escape the appetites of its own unsentimental brethren to ripen into a nocturnal nuisance (an estimated five years to reach sexual maturity), well, that was purely marvelous. Furthermore, that it could propel a gulp of air across its vocal chords to produce a vibration of such magnitude that it could be heard up to a mile away without even opening its mouth? Positively supernatural. But yes, the plain fact of it kept me awake too.

How can we explain this? How can we understand this? More to the point, how can we ignore this?

The love song of the *Rana catesbeiana*, the American bullfrog, is the song of enlightenment. It is uncontrived, utterly natural, as it is. It has a trillion verses. It isn't written. It isn't known. It never stops. It never starts. It has no sound but every sound, no form but every form. It is the streaming, pounding pulse of a thousand million stars. The silent drum of dew dropping from a billion blades of grass in your front yard. The poetry of dragonflies, all motion, no meaning, spun from the beat of the heat on an August afternoon. The sigh in a pine. A ripple in the air. The roar from this old croaker — *me!* — reverberating through the darkness to wake you up — *wake up!* — without even opening her mouth.

Life is a lyric you don't write and a tune you don't know. It's spontaneous: happening right now. Completely original: yours and yours alone. Unceasing and yet as ephemeral as spring. Do you hear it? Can you ever *not* hear it?

"It's a frog," I said. The answer, like all answers, would do nothing to ease his affliction. "Even with earplugs you can't drown it out."

As a girl of four or five, staying overnight at the old place, I slept with my grandfather. He could snore like a bear, but I never heard him snore, or at least I was never troubled by it. What I heard at night, through the screen door, atop the dark chill that carried the flavor of freshness, were the crickets.

I just heard the crickets.

I didn't make any meaning of it then — four-year-olds don't yet assign meaning to things — and I don't make any meaning of it now.

I simply heard the crickets. I knew they were crickets and I knew where I was and how I was and what time it was and what it was time to do. I knew everything that you know when you hear a cricket, which is actually quite a bit, so much that you can't really explain it all. And the good thing is, you don't have to.

I'm reciting all this because lately when I toss in bed, I

can remember what I knew for sure when I was a little girl. Now my head is crowded with far more than it needs to be — fear, for instance, of being old, and worry, and doubts about my work, especially this work, and my daughter and whether she will be okay and not too disappointed or hurt and then the prescription that needs refilling and the bills that need to be paid and I forgot, what did I forget, oh, that's right I forgot to call, to fix, to sign, to return, to finish, to start — and for all I know there are crickets outside my own window right now, but most of the time I'm making far too much noise between my ears to hear them.

That's what can come between a sound and a song, between the lost and the found, and between the solid earth and the endless sky. That's all there is to let go of: what we keep putting in between.

There are infinite gates to the garden, and they are all open, without interruption or delay. Frogs and dogs, dragonflies and crickets, wind and weeds: all can pass through to paradise. Why, oh, why can't you?

"It helps to be stupid," Maezumi said. Not knowing is most intimate. Most profound. Most true. There is no *why* except the one blocking your ears.

Yes, but when are you going to teach me something about Zen?

When are you going to tell me how to become a Buddhist? What to believe? What to say, what to do, where to go? The ten rules? The eight ways? The hidden doctrine, the secret handshake, the first principle of the holy teaching?

Once I started practicing, it didn't take me long to realize that this path was my salvation. The tip-off was that I was still alive. Leaving a retreat, I called a friend who had been kind enough to show me how to sit. I was ready to make a pronouncement, and I wanted her to hear it first.

"I'm a Buddhist!" I said. She didn't give me one minute to boast.

"One more thing to let go of." For a Buddhist, you see, there's always one more thing to let go of. Let go of being a Buddhist, and you just might become one. Don't enrobe your ego in one more layer of identity — one more name, one more definition, one more set of expectations. They are meaningless. Deep down you already know how to live, and how not to live. You've already heard the truth, and you know a lie when you hear yourself tell one. You've already seen the Way, and you know when you have lost it. You weren't born with missing parts, absent a set of instructions. You have an intuitive guidance system, and it is flawless. You don't need directions, even though it can be useful to consult them until you no longer confuse the road map for the road. We have to let go of everything we think we know — all the concepts and intellectualizations — because human knowledge is limited to the brain, but human wisdom is not. You are much, much more than whatever it is you call *yourself*. Turn your attention away from yourself and do something good instead. You know how to do good. Do it right where you are.

These days there is a scientific initiative to explore the human brain. Using neuroscience and nanotechnology, scientists, philosophers, and clergy are discussing how to "map the mind." They want to find the biological origin of wisdom and locate the neural patterns of empathy and compassion, so that human beings can learn how to do the right thing. Some Buddhists liken this undertaking to an evolutionary leap on the path to enlightenment, a breakthrough unavailable to Buddha, who labored so primitively in his quest without the insight of neurobiology or the guidance of brain imaging. Just imagine how much farther we can go in the twenty-first century, the argument goes. Indeed, imaginations run wild.

Except this: the map of the mind is the universe beneath your feet. All of time is contained in this moment. Nothing and nowhere is farther than here and now. I'll leave all the excitement about the future to folks smarter than I. I have more than enough right here. I have a frog to teach me the mysteries of mind. He lectures me every night.

If you study with a mapmaker you'll learn to draw a map. I studied with a wayfarer and learned the Way. It keeps going. It covers every place on earth and reaches every inch of sky. Perhaps we'll meet like minstrels along the road and share our songs. I'd like that.

In his recorded talks, Maezumi Roshi had handed me what appeared to be relics, encoded in obsolescence, encrypted in a dead language. The last batch of tapes he sent were talks on the Ten Oxherding Pictures, a classical Zen teaching device that originated during the Song Dynasty of twelfth-century China. The simple drawings illustrate the sequence of steps we timid herders must take to tame a wild mind — the ox — and realize the ease and freedom of our true nature. Of course, appearing to be simple doesn't make it simple to do. He gave these talks just a few months before he died, and hurried to send them to me; a publisher was waiting. What would I make of them?

Alas, I made nothing. I've never even listened to them all. I was not particularly clever or ambitious. There was so much life that came my way — new people, circumstances, and priorities. Sickness, trouble, setbacks, and suffering. Lately, one of the pictures has come to mind, at night. It's late summer as I write this, and the song of the frog is at its climax. I wake often.

In this picture, the seeking is over. The ox herder has chased, found, reined in, and tamed the wayward bull. Now he hoists himself atop the domesticated beast and lets it carry him home. The two move as one; there is no conflict or hurry. The rider isn't leading the way. He isn't even holding the reins; he's holding a flute! Sitting *backward* on the slow-moving ox, he gazes up at the drifting clouds and plays a children's song, unconcerned with where the road will go. And thus he completes his journey.

When your faith is secure, you will never be lost. Then who needs to learn the way home?

I have had great teachers, and they teach me still. The hallmark of great teachers is their complete disinterest in your qualifications. They do not measure your ability or evaluate your prospects. They never judge you. They do not educate or explain. They do not proselytize. They keep company with you in a place beyond names and a time that never ends: in *samadhi*, nondistracted awareness. The place you go to meet them is your own emptied mind, illuminated with compassion, the light within which all afflictions dissolve. If you think you don't have an emptied mind, look around until you realize that it's been here all along, appearing as it is. If you wonder where the light is, it's the light with which you see these words.

I have nothing to add to what doesn't need to be said, so I'll quote one of the last things Maezumi taught me.

"When you really see it, realize it, you don't need to say even a word!"

It's time for me to stop drawing pictures on the surface of the old pond, where the moon already shines and the frog preaches the living truth as clear as a temple bell.

CHAPTER 18

SILENCE
Not What I Say

A special transmission outside the scriptures;
No dependence upon words and letters;
Direct pointing to the mind of man:
Seeing into one's own nature and attaining buddhahood.
— BODHIDHARMA

We came here in the summer, and now it's sixteen summers later. The place has grown on us. Not long ago we called the Japanese garden guy we first consulted when we wanted to know how to restore the yard to her glory. What he said then set us back a step. We weren't prepared to go that far, so we made our way alone. But now it's our turn to repay what we owe to the gardeners who came before us.

The master is old now. He travels in a wheelchair. Once in the backyard, he sits still and quiet for three hours conceiving the plan. When he reveals it, nothing he says is untrue. All of it is good and necessary, obvious to an experienced eye.

Locate the source and repair the water lines.

Secure the rocks.

Prune the dead.

Trim the overgrowth.

Replant the perennials.

Clear the paths.

Open the sight lines.

Raise the lantern, and let the visitors come.

My husband and I look at each other. Our eyes meet in silent accord. The scope of the job is exactly what we feared. It will cost a lot of money, but we know what we will do. We will do what is required, and when we leave, it will be done.

Is it reckless to deplete your resources simply to prepare the garden for the next pilgrim? Yes, but that's what a gardener does. Enter a treasure like this, and you'll know that your time here is a gift. In return, your investment must be total. The future of all living things comes down to what you will do while you are here.

What will you do? First, don't take my word alone as the truth. My words only point to paradise, the paradise waiting for you to bring to life. No garden looks like any other. Yours may not even be a garden. It may be a cracked sidewalk on a busy street, beside a river of roaring cars, headlights streaming nonstop into a noisy night. Your paradise may be in a desert without a bloom, a kitchen without a window, a house now absent of love and laughter, short on the days and seasons you thought would last forever.

I can only say this: *me too*. We are not so different from one another, any of us. There is one mind and we share it. One Way and we walk it. One path and it leads straight on. To see the whole of it, you have to keep going, and then keep going some more. When you come to the open ground, what will you plant? When will you tend it? How will you leave it?

My teachers taught me to leave no trace, so here's my last chance to sweep up after myself.

Forget everything I've said. Your life is the life of the entire universe. How can I add a single thing to it?

I wish I could say there was no discord in Zen. That there were no debates about substance or meaning, historical accuracy, and literal truth. That there was no cynicism about enlightenment, disputes about the way the teaching comes down to you and me.

It comes like this.

The origin of Zen is attributed to an Indian meditation master named Bodhidharma, who brought the Buddha's original teaching to northern China. Some say he came by water, some say by ground, around the end of the fifth century, give or take. His passage was tossed by storms yet favored by winds. He was chased by bandits and aided by strangers. Eventually he found a place to stay. He erected a sanctuary, made his mind like a mountain wall, and turned his gaze inward. There he planted a seed that rooted a tree that bears fruit in my own backyard. I can taste it.

But some scholars doubt his existence. They argue that Bodhidharma didn't do what he was said to do, or say the words attributed to him. Some say the lineage of Zen teachers — from China to Japan to the West and thus to the here and now — is a ruse. That the stories are myth and the teachers phony, the entire tradition just the handiwork of spiritual schemers.

This garden too has its detractors who doubt the authenticity of the rock where I stand.

Disagreement is the nature of human delusion, but it is not the nature of nature. The earth does not argue with the sky, the ocean does not resist the rain, and the clouds do not refuse the wind. A single day in the garden will clear your mind of intellectual disturbance.

About this my teacher is compassionately swift. "Who cares who said the words if they are true? Who cares how the teaching came if it is here?" The responsibility to awaken is ours alone, and no matter where the dharma comes from, each of us has everything we need to get the job done. We can depend on no one and nothing else.

I've shown you the gate and the signposts. Now you know how to locate the path. I've pointed to the sun and moon that light your way. Now you know where to stand, what to prune, how to plant, and when to weed. You have the time. You have the instincts. I've handed you a hoe. Now put on your hat, and be off.

Don't worry about a thing. It's the garden that makes the gardener, not the other way around. All you have to do is show up. Even when I'm gone from sight, I'll keep you silent company, like all the gardeners before me. Where else is there to go?

⟨∾⟩

At the beginning of this book I said I was talking to you, but I've only been muttering to myself. You thought you were hearing my words, but all along you were speaking them to yourself. The two of us have entered a profound intimacy, a state of oneness, in total silence. No time or distance, no shape or sound: nothing separates us. This is Buddha mind, awakened mind, and it is the Way of all the ancestors.

During a three-month *ango*, or training period, a novice monk is selected to serve as the head trainee at the monastery. He or she will monitor the practice inside the meditation hall, acting as a model and mentor for those who join in. The monk maintains order, harmony, motivation, and discipline through the depth of his or her own *samadhi*.

Nowadays there aren't many Zen monks, but anyone can become a Zen student just by entering the gate.

A simple ceremony marks the beginning of the training period, when the student formally enters the temple to begin the term of service. The trainee and the teacher will commence a long stretch of silence sitting side by side in *zazen*, doing their work alone and together. The student will swim through a flood of fear and crawl over a mountain of doubt. The work will consume light and dark, days and nights on end. At first he will cherish nothing more than the thought of escape, but in time he will plant himself deep in the ground and give up the search. On the last day of training, the student will enter a place he has never been. It will be in the exact same place he's never left, but the walls will be gone, a cramped and airless room transformed into a garden of living things. He will know perfectly well how to take good care of it.

But this is still the first day, and he has no idea where the path is leading.

Ceremonies in the zendo are orchestrated, the script ordained in the manner of a thousand students and a hundred teachers before. The student stands before the teacher and expresses humility and gratitude. He moves to make his bows, but the teacher waves him off. There is no need for formality between them, no show of rank. The two are fellow travelers, and they will make this trip as one.

With palms together, the student speaks the last public words that will pass between them until they reach the other side. The room is quiet. Nothing stirs. Paradise comes into view.

"California weather is peaceful and calm. May your days go well."

Since then, the poet has come to set these things first of all: to lift up his eyes and see the mountains; to lower them and listen to the stream; to look about him at bamboos, willows, clouds, and rocks, from morn till nightfall. One night's lodging brings rest to the body; two nights give peace to the heart; after three nights the drooping and depressed no longer know either trouble. If one asked the reason, the answer is simply — the place.

— Po Chu-i (772–864)

RULES FOR A MINDFUL GARDEN

Indra took a blade of grass and stuck it in the ground and said, "The sanctuary has been erected." Buddha smiled.

— BOOK OF SERENITY, CASE 4

These are the rules I give to groups of children when they visit the garden. The rules apply to us all, but they are easier for children to follow than adults.

1. *Be kind.* Every time we are kind to another, we are kind to ourselves, because we have left our self-centeredness behind. It's important: kindness is the supreme religion. It's not hard: pure silence is the ultimate kindness. We already know how to do it.

2. *Don't throw rocks.* The garden path is paved with stones. It's tempting for children to pick one up and loft it into the ponds. It's tempting for adults to pick one up and loft it at someone else. When we blame others and the circumstances around us

for whatever displeases us, we are tossing rocks. To maintain peace in your garden, don't pick up a rock if you can't set it down.

3. *No running.* There's no hurry, and no one is chasing you. Running is a sure way to fall into the murky mud beneath you. How much of life do we miss because we are racing headfirst toward someplace else, a place we never reach? You have all the time in the world to appreciate the life you have.

4. *Pay attention.* Bring all your attention to what is in front of you. You'll wake up to the view and realize you're right at home where you are.

ACKNOWLEDGMENTS

I would like to thank:

My real estate agent, Judy Webb-Martin, for taking me outside my parameters, and my literary agent, Ted Weinstein, for reminding me that I'm here.

My first reader, author Katrina Kenison, for laughing when I laugh and crying when I cry.

My husband and daughter for insisting that I take a backward step, and my dog, Molly, for insisting that I take a forward step.

My grandfathers: George James Tate, for showing me how to peel an orange, and Otto Paul Patschke, for showing me how to whistle.

The gardeners: Tokutaro Kato, Thomasella Graham, Maezumi Roshi, Tomás Ramirez, Sam Moriyama, Jeffery Isobe, Arturo Garcia, and Lew Watanabe.

The sanghas at Hazy Moon Zen Center in Los Angeles, Rime Buddhist Center in Kansas City, Lil Omm in Washington, D.C., NatureBridge in San Francisco, and Grailville in Ohio for inviting me to sit down.

Martha Ekyo Maezumi for her trust and permission.

My teacher, Nyogen Roshi, for everything.

PERMISSIONS

To carry the self forward and realize the ten thousand things is delusion.
That the ten thousand things come forth and realize the self is enlightenment.
— DOGEN ZENJI

Zen is a living tradition, conveyed in a moment of time as real as this one. While a student can come to his or her own insights only through personal practice, the words of the masters point the way to wakefulness.

Those words can arise in conversations, such as the ones that appear at the beginning of some chapters in this book, as "cases," or koans. Koans are records of encounters between enlightened teachers and students who lived during the Tang Dynasty (618–907) in China. These oft-repeated stories were compiled during the Song Dynasty (960–1279) into written collections, which are still used in Zen training.

Or a teaching may have been expressed in verse, written on rocks, bamboo, walls, or paper, and left behind.

Dharma words arise spontaneously, are spoken or written, then are lost, found, forgotten, remembered, and recited. That even a single phrase I've quoted on these pages endures to this day is as miraculous as a blade of grass growing through a crack in the sidewalk. I am therefore grateful to the following translators, editors, and publishers for permission to use passages from these important works:

Koan cases of *The Gateless Gate* (pages 9, 25, 33, and 67) and *Blue Cliff Record* (pages 49 and 149) are excerpted from *Two Zen Classics*, translated and with commentaries by Katsuki Sekida. Copyright © Katsuki Sekida and A. V. Grimstone. Reprinted by arrangement with the Permissions Company, Inc., on behalf of Shambhala Publications, Inc., Boston, MA, www.shambhala.com.

Writings of Dogen Zenji (pages 39, 97, 102, 129, and 169) are excerpted from *Moon in a Dewdrop* by Dogen, translated by Kazuaki Tanahashi. Translation copyright © San Francisco Zen Center. Reprinted with permission of North Point Press, a division of Farrar, Straus and Giroux, LLC.

The poetry of Dogen Zenji (page vii) is taken from *A Blade of Grass: Japanese Poetry and Aesthetics in Dogen Zen* by Steven Heine. Copyright © Steven Heine. Reprinted with permission of the author.

A passage from *The Record of Transmitting the Light* by Keizan Zenji (page 3) was translated by Francis H. Cook. Copyright © Zen Center of Los Angeles. Reprinted with permission of Wisdom Publications, www.wisdom publications.org.

The record of Po Chu-i (page 163) is excerpted from *The*

ABOUT THE AUTHOR

Karen Maezen Miller is a Zen Buddhist priest and teacher at the Hazy Moon Zen Center in Los Angeles. She is the author of *Hand Wash Cold: Care Instructions for an Ordinary Life* and *Momma Zen: Walking the Crooked Path of Motherhood*. She leads retreats around the country. Contact her at www.karenmaezenmiller.com.